MEAN
girls

facing your beauty turned beast

Hayley DiMarco

pinkmosphere
a part of Hungry Planet

Revell
Grand Rapids, Michigan

Published by Fleming H. Revell
a division of Baker Publishing Group
P.O. Box 6287, Grand Rapids, MI 49516-6287
www.revellbooks.com

Printed in the United States of America

Library of Congress Cataloging-in-Publication Data is on file at the Library
of Congress, Washington, D.C.

Published in association with Yates & Yates, LLP, Literary Agents, Orange, California.

Contents

You and Your Mean Girl

Choosing Beauty Over the Beast
The Girl Grown Up

Mean Friends

School of the Unmean

Ammo for the Battle

www.meangirls.net

My Story

If you have a Mean Girl in your life, I understand more than you might know how horrible you feel right now. You hate getting up in the morning because you know that as soon as you get to school or work, she will be there. Leering at you, laughing at you, thinking about you, *talking* about you. You don't know what she'll do next or where she will be. Oh yes, I know that feeling all too well because my high school years were plagued with Mean Girls.

In my class of 40 people, I was the victim of choice for the popular crowd. For 4 years I hated going to school. I sat in class day in and day out and watched them plot and plan to hurt me. I tried to make friends, but in the end even they turned against me in one way or another. The kiss of death for me (which might have some of you rolling your eyes) was that all the boys liked me. I was really shy and so I guess kind of mysterious. I also wasn't a sexually active girl, so, boys being boys, they all wanted to get the virgin. (News flash: They never did!)

I was continually the subject of all kinds of plots. If I was dating a guy, they wanted to get him from me. If I had a nice car, they wanted to ruin it. If my mom trusted me, they wanted her to stop trusting me. One day a pair of panties was placed in our mailbox as if someone was returning them to me after a night of passion. What a joke. Torturing me was quite a sport for them, though. Every day when I left school I would find a big wad of spit on the hood of my car. Every day, without fail. I hated walking out to my car as they all laughed at me. I can remember being afraid to go to the bathroom because I might meet one of them in there alone, and that would be devastating.

When I started dating a guy that one of them wanted to date, they not only TP'd his house but also spray painted his driveway with bad things about *me*. They were bent on making me look bad. When our Sadie Hawkins dance (girls ask guys) came along, one of the girls asked my boyfriend before I could (of course, he was a stupid boy for saying yes, but that's beside the current point).

I thought I had found sanctuary in those friends I told you about, but they soon turned on me as well. **Why is it that girls think that boys are more important than their friends?** My friend made out with my new love the day after he and I got together. I was shocked, but I guess I shouldn't have been. After all, friends aren't as important as boys. Ugh!

All this meanness finally culminated in one horrible act that freaked me out and made me fear for my safety. One day in my senior year I went to my locker, and as I opened it I saw a small noose with something hanging from it. It was soft and slimy like a dead finger. A note that hung from the rope said, "Beware the DOA." Needless to say, it totally freaked me out. I slammed the locker and ran to the school office. **This was too much.** Until that time I hadn't said anything to anyone, but this looked like something that should be taken more seriously.

When the principal went back to check my locker, she found that what was hanging there was a peeled carrot, carved like a person. Apparently it had been left in the freezer overnight so that now it was cold, clammy, and limp. Pretty ingenious girls!

I was devastated that their hatred of me had gone that far. I don't know for sure why the girls decided that I was archenemy number one, but I was. Was it because I was shy? Was I aloof in my shyness? I'll never know, but my high school years were tainted by the treatment of a handful of angry teenage girls.

I always thought they had no idea what they were doing to me—until years later when I found out the truth. I was at a party with a bunch of friends from high school, and one of the Mean Girls was there too. She pulled me aside and said, "We treated you really bad in school and did some really mean things. I'm sorry about what we did." I thought that was a really nice and noble thing to do, so I smiled and said, "Oh, don't worry about it. We were young; it's okay. I forgive you." She looked at me in shock, her mouth open, and said, "Oh, great. Why'd you have to be so nice even now? It would have been much easier if you would have been mean about it!" Even then, my kindness was killing her. Maybe that's what they mean by "kill 'em with kindness."

I didn't learn to trust girls for years after high school. I spent most of my college and adult years, until a few years ago, only being close to guys. I just couldn't handle the "girl scene," as I liked to call it. "They are just so catty and mean. I don't like 'em. Guys are easygoing, not vindictive or petty. I prefer guys," I used to say. But now that I have healed from my experiences and started to see the truth, I can say that I love girls. In fact, I *need* girls. If it weren't for girls, I would be really messed up. Let's face it, we need each other. Guys are great, sure, but they are different, and you can't really connect with a guy the same way you can connect with a girl.

Now I can sit up all night with my girlfriends, talking about guys. I can talk their ears off and never feel like I'm boring them. I can shop all day with my girlfriends. I can share clothes with them. Tell my secrets to them. Confide in them. And nurture them. Girls bring out the girl in me, and that's pretty cool. Because when you get right down to it, it's the girl in you that guys are attracted to, not the guy in you. I didn't understand that till many years after high school. I was so busy trying not to be like the Mean Girls that I became like a guy and totally gave up my girlyness. And it wasn't until I decided I really wanted a man and was ready to think of the "M" word that I found out I really needed girls.

See, my dears, guys will never replace girls. They weren't meant to. Most guys don't need to talk as much as girls, so we need backup friends to use all our words on. Guys, on the whole, don't like shopping as much either, so we need girls to fill that void. And most guys definitely don't like sharing all their hopes, fears, and emotions with us all the time like we want to, but girls do, and I thank God for that. My mom always told me, "Hayley, whenever you start dating someone, don't stop seeing your girlfriends. You need them. If you dump them and expect him to take their place, you'll be in big trouble. He just can't do it. He's a guy. Save all your girl emotions and traumas for girls who get it. And just enjoy the guy." Women who are wise know that even after you get married, keeping your girlfriends is essential. Guys and girls both need "me" time, and a girlfriend is a good sounding board and confidante for your emotions and dreams.

So don't give up on girls just yet. We are fun. We have fun together. We bond in ways guys never can. And besides, you need someone to get your back, to tell you when your jeans are too short or your belt doesn't match your shoes or, worse yet, when you have something in your teeth. Ah, girls. They are great. Don't let a few mean ones taint it for the rest of us. Find a girlfriend or two and make a good relationship that will last a lifetime.

When I was a teenager, my spirit was imprisoned by fear, maybe like yours is right now. I had no sense of the greatness of God or the power of his hand in my life. I couldn't see life from his point of view, only from my weak little place on the planet. I didn't understand a bigger picture because I had not yet discovered Christ and his teachings, his Spirit, and his love. I didn't come to understand that until after college. If I had known *then* what I know *now*, maybe those girls would have ended up my friends or at least left me alone a little bit. No one ever told me how to handle them, what to say to them, or how to be around them. Instead I was just plain scared of them. I lived a lot of my life in fear, and it didn't have to be that way. How sad that no one was there to tell me about the amazing truth of godliness with love. Now that I have come through years of fighting with the Mean Girl and of not knowing how to avoid her or get rid of her, I have a new understanding of how I am supposed to react to her, even if I can't get rid of her.

I wrote *Mean Girls* to help you better understand who you are so that you can stop the Mean Girl cycle. This book will help you to find your destiny and live in it as a graceful spiritual girl. *Mean Girls* will help you face the beauty in the beast of your Mean Girl and maybe even find a way to change a generation of Mean Girls from the inside out. What you learn in this book might shock you. It might even tick you off, but don't stop. If you want to get to the bottom of your pain, then you have to power through. On the other side is hope and a life filled with peace and love. Mean Girls might be around you forever, but they might never affect you again if you follow the principles in this book and remain honest with and true to yourself.

The Beast

The Mean Girl. The beast. The one who tears at your flesh and devours your heart. She growls when you walk by. She hisses as you leave. She probably drools over you in her sleep. She's a beast all right, plain and simple. It's evident in all she is and all she does. So what do you do with this beast in your life? Can you find a hint of hope, or are you destined to spend your life running in fear from this rabid female? Oh, my dear, the answer is near. Come with me on a journey through the bizarre. Join me in scrutinizing the female psyche and follow me to a land of freedom and hope.

Girls have become the most catty, manipulative, emotional people on the planet, and you are at their mercy. Or are you? At one time I didn't see a way out, so weak was my faith. But now I do. I believe that the Mean Girl can be a thing of the past. I believe that her power over you will diminish and that your victories will be many. Your bruises will heal and your cuts will mend. *Mean Girls* is a call to spiritual strength. A call to stand firm. It is a call to face the beasts in your life head-on and with faithful resolve. And it is the answer that you've been looking for. Mean Girls . . . shall we attempt to find the beauty in your beast?

Why This Book Works

This book is full of some powerful stuff that is guaran-teed to help you with the Mean Girls in your life if you are willing to live by it.

This isn't for the faint of heart.

It isn't self-help for the brave or the strong.

It's about a way of life based on the truth offered by a best-selling book called the Bible.

Conquering the mean in your life is only going to work if you have a power bigger than yourself working alongside you, above you, and in you. And I hope that by the end of this book you will know a little bit more about this life-changing power that tramples mean.

Warning: You might find some tips and tricks in here that make perfect sense, and you might try them and find that life gets a little bit better—but without faith in a God who can change lives and change hearts, any change will only be temporary.

So let's dive into the realm of mean

and see if we can't find real beauty.

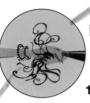

Do You Have a Mean Girl Problem?

Answer the following to find out.

1. When you walk down the hall, most of the time you are:

  a. alone

  b. with your gang

  c. with your best bud

2. Sometimes you:

  a. get laughed at by other girls

  b. make fun of the not-so-popular girl's clothes

  c. hang with your friends and have so much fun you forget it's time to go

3. You know how it feels to:

  a. be gossiped about

  b. make someone look bad so you look good

  c. care for a friend who is hurt

4. You spend hours:

  a. worrying about how not to be seen by other girls

  b. thinking about how to get even with someone

  c. helping your friends through tough times

5. When you go to school, you are:

  a. afraid to go to the bathroom alone

  b. lovin' life

  c. counseling your friends about all their problems

6. Your parents:

  a. would say you worry a lot about going to school

  b. know that you are happiest when you are with your friends

  c. taught you how to care for others

7. At least once a week:
    a. another girl laughs at you or picks on you
    b. you talk about another girl in a way that puts her down
    c. you try to make your friend feel really good about herself

8. You have cried at school:
    a. many times
    b. only occasionally when a guy is a jerk
    c. not really at all, because you save that for your bedroom

Now add up your scores:

A = 3
B = 2
C = 1

18-24: **MG problems.** You probably have to deal with at least one girl who is out to get you. This book will help you learn more about her and how to handle yourself when she freaks out on you. Don't worry, this won't last forever. This trauma you are living in has an end. Keep the faith.

11-17: **MG.** Did you ever think that you might be the Mean Girl of someone's nightmares? This quiz isn't a perfect diagnosis, but you might want to read on to find out who you are when others are looking.

8-10: **No MG for you.** You probably are the one helping the victims of MGs. You see the pain they cause but have mostly stayed free from their attacks. You'll be in a great place if you can learn more about them so you can help more than you do right now. You are the key to solving the troubles between these girls. Never stop being faithful.

the
Mean
Girl

Mean for Fun (aka *Really Mean Girls*)

You see her at the other end of the hall. Your stomach rolls over and thinks about climbing up your throat. The Mean Girl. The one whose job it is to torture you. As you walk closer she begins to whisper to her friends while she stares at you. They giggle and all look at you at once. The humiliation brings the blood to your cheeks. If only you could hide the pain, but it's out there for all to see. As you walk past them, you pull your books in to your chest for protection. You feel the sharp pain of knives driving into your back, and you wince. What have you done? Why do they hate you? What will they do next? And who will believe them?

Really Mean Girls define themselves based on who they can hurt. It's a power trip. Their goal in life. It gives them satisfaction to see you squirm. It makes them feel good when you get mad at them. And it makes them look good to all their friends when they point out how pathetic you are. They don't need any other reason. It's not what you've done; it's how really mean they've become. Their mean is just for fun.

So what do you do with Mean Girls?

How do you get around them or change them?

Will your life forever be plagued by females who hate other females?

What is the cause of her stupid attitude?

Is it something you have done?

So many questions

And so many answers in *Mean Girls: Facing Your Beauty Turned Beast*. Take a walk with me through the wild side of Mean Girls.

Mean for a Reason

The girl who is *Mean for Fun,* she's easy to spot. We all wish she would just leave us alone. But there is another Mean Girl out there. She's the one who is *Mean for a Reason.* Check her out:

The big dance is this weekend. You can hardly wait. Your man is so cute, and he is all about you. You two are going to have a total blast. When you get there, things are going great. The music is pumpin', your friends are with you, and he's as cute as ever. You dance a few songs and then go to get something to drink. In the shuffle your guy ends up on the other side of the gym without you. That's okay, you'll get him on the next song. As you wind your way back toward the dance floor, your best friend says, "Hey, isn't that your guy dancing with that girl?"

You turn to focus in on the man of your dreams locked arm in arm with her. As you watch, the most horrific thing imaginable happens—they start staring into each other's eyes. It's major chemistry. They are locked together, barely swaying to the music. Then it happens. It's only a brush, but their lips come together. Your friends start to moan and scream. It's over. He's toast. But her? She's dead!

Horrible feeling, huh? I hate just reading it. Okay, now check out this list. Circle True or False for how you felt when you read this little story. If that story happened to me:

The girl would be history, because revenge
  is sweet.   True   False

That girl had no right to do that with
  my guy.   True   False

I'd figure out how to get her back.   True   False

I would give my guy the cold shoulder for a couple
    weeks. **True** **False**

I'd never trust that girl again. **True** **False**

I think it's the girl's fault. **True** **False**

If you answered true to any of these, you might just be a Mean Girl in disguise. A *Mean Girl for a Reason*. Sure, you feel justified—I mean, *she* started it. But then when does it end? You get her back and then suddenly you're *her* Mean Girl. She gets you back, so now *she's* the Mean Girl, and the cycle goes on. Do you really want revenge that bad? Is revenge more important to you than happiness? Because you know that revenge doesn't end well; it always keeps the anger flowing between you and the enemy. In fact, it gets between you and God as well. He tells us that vengeance is his (see the apostle Paul's letters to the Romans, chapter 12, verse 19), and taking what is God's doesn't sit so well, so beware when you decide that you can take revenge yourself. And besides, his vengeance is better for changing people from mean to good than yours could ever be.

So you have a choice: You can choose to stop the insanity where it is, or you can jump in, take over, and drive that puppy to the ground.

To see what happens when you do keep the revenge alive, check out page 80, *The Mean Girl Cycle*.

Degrees of Mean

You're probably reading this book because you've got a Mean Girl in your life. And if you do, then you probably want to get rid of her. She has many tools in her arsenal, and she knows how to use them. So what do you do in order to stop her attacks? How do you react to her jabs, her slices, her stabs? The way you react will determine her next attack, so be very careful, and you might be able to get away from your Mean Girl unscathed.

The Gossip Girl

For girls, gossip is the currency that buys you a place in another girl's heart. It's bonding. You know the feeling. When you tell a friend something you heard or saw and you know you shouldn't be repeating it, you feel the endorphins running through your blood, almost giving you a little buzz. It's a great feeling, and you become soul sisters. *"What dainty morsels rumors are—but they sink deep into one's heart"* (from the ancient book of Proverbs in the Bible, chapter 18, verse 8, NLT). Gossip, ah, how refreshing! And you know that as soon as the popular girl wants to tell you some big G, then you're in. Gossip gets you into the "in" crowd, and it makes you part of the "family." Without gossip, most girls wouldn't have anything to talk about.

And for Mean Girls, gossip is the preferred weapon of choice. They love it. It makes them feel good and others feel bad; it's a perfect weapon containing both pleasure and pain. But its destructive powers are worse than its pleasures ever could be. A lot of us gossip, but we don't really do it to be mean; we just do it because, well, what else is there to talk about besides other people? It's almost like a requirement. You wanna be friends, you gotta share juicy G. But more than a fun way to bond with your best friends, it's a sin in the face of God (according to the Bible's

Common sense indicates that 99.99% of girls gossip.

> A gossip tells secrets, so don't hang around with someone who talks too much.
> —King Solomon*

book of Leviticus, chapter 19, verse 16). And not only is it a sin, but it's a sin that deeply hurts the subject of the gossip party. In fact, it can totally destroy the object of its attention. And Mean Girls know that. They use gossip like it's a machine gun, shooting down every girl they have it in for. And if there isn't anything true to talk about, they'll make it up.

When a girl gossips, it doesn't have to be the truth. It just has to sound good and juicy. The thing to remember is that the gossip isn't only about you; it's also about her bonding with her friends, as sick as that is. You can't keep it from hurting, but you can keep it from destroying you.

1. **Ignore her.** Don't give her any reaction. Ignore her lies. Ignore her words. See, her goal is to make you mad. When she gets her goal, it's like she gets extra lives on her video game, and she just keeps coming back for more battles. Always keep in mind, what is the goal of the game? The Mean Girl's goal, is to get a reaction out of you. When you do your best to ignore it, gossip loses its value and girls lose their interest in it. We can find the wisdom behind this truth in an ancient proverb written by King Solomon, which goes something like this: *"A fool shows her annoyance at once, but a smart girl overlooks an insult"* (the book of Proverbs chapter 12, verse 16, *Mean Girls* paraphrase). It's an ancient truth: **Ignore it and you help it go away.**

Some girls will never lose interest in hurting you, but you can't control that beyond doing what you are called to do. Follow your calling and live with the outcome.

Okay, so how do you do that? Glad you asked, my darling. Ignoring gossip has more to do with acting like you've ignored it than really ignoring it. I mean, face it, it's hard to really ignore it and go on, but it's easier to *act*

*The book of Proverbs 20:19 NLT

like you didn't even notice it and then go home and cry. When you hear about the rumor, don't get upset, at least not in public, and definitely not in front of her! I repeat, *don't get upset.* Don't yell at your friend, "But that just isn't true!" or storm up to the gossiper and give her a piece of your mind. That is not ignoring it. That is playing right into her game. Mean Girls love to see you squirm; it's why they do what they do. So never let 'em see you squirm.

I bet your mom tried to teach you this when you were a kid and you never really believed her. "Don't pay attention to your brother and he'll stop picking on you," she said. This isn't a family cliché for nothing. It's the truth. When you stop giving someone a reaction, they are much more likely to get bored than if you play the game with them. It's like that game Whack-a-Mole at the arcade, where you hit the little mole heads that pop up from holes on a table. When you hit them with a mallet, they disappear in their holes. The goal is to hit them as quickly as they come up. It's addictive because they keep popping back up. Now think how boring the game would be if they never went in their holes once you hit them or never popped back up once they went down. You'd get really bored really fast and walk away to play some other game. It's the same with the Mean Girl. If she can't get you to keep popping back in and out of your hole, she gets bored.

Note: Unfortunately, every rule has an exception, and with Mean Girls it's no different. Some girls will never give up, never leave you alone, no matter how you respond. But that shouldn't change your response. That doesn't make ignoring her jabs a bad thing; it just makes her way messed up. Your job as a believer,

Her number one goal is to get a reaction out of you—to make you mad.

no matter what, is to love her and pray for her as if she is your friend. (See *Changing a Mean Girl* on page 93.) And to God, loving someone means overlooking an offense. King Solomon said in the book of Proverbs, chapter 19, verse 11, *"A man's wisdom gives him patience; it is to his glory to overlook an offense."* Ignore it and you've followed the will of God and overlooked an offense.

2. Prove her wrong. The second thing you can do when a Gossip Girl strikes is to prove her wrong. Think about the tabloid the *Globe* versus the *New York Times*. The stories in the *Globe* are so far-fetched and ridiculous that no one believes them anymore. It's a trash magazine, one you read just to get a good laugh over the two-headed baby or the space alien who kidnapped Britney Spears and replaced her with a double. But the *New York Times* gets their stories right most of the time. They are respected as a good source of news. So when the Gossip Girl says stuff about you that isn't true, she loses points if you prove her wrong. Let's say she says that you are a total whore and will sleep with anyone. Now, first off, you aren't actually a whore, so already she's wrong. But anyone who knows you also knows that you don't sleep around. And even if you did slip and fool around with a guy, which is why she is gossiping about you, you can prove her wrong by never letting that happen again. And you win. In the end she gets to be like the *Globe*—she'll always have an audience who wants to hear the latest lie, but she is still a trashy tabloid that no one takes seriously. (The Bible agrees: 1 Peter chapter 2, verse 12; Proverbs chapter 20, verse 3; Proverbs chapter 19, verse 11.)

So to win the gossip game, ignore the Gossip Girl and prove her wrong. Game point: You win. Play the game right, and your gossip nightmare could disappear.

Check out more about the Gossip Hound, the friend who loves to gossip, in *How to Handle Your Mean Friends*, page 151.

Why it makes us feel better to call someone else a name is beyond me, but it does. It just seems to make you feel good to call someone else a name when you're mad at them. And Mean Girls love feeling better about themselves by calling you names. Here's the thing: You don't even have to be what she says for her to call you it. You might be tall and skinny, and she will call you an Amazon woman. And even though you aren't an Amazon woman, you still feel hurt. Why? Because you think that someone thinks badly of you, and that hurts. Believe me, I know. I've been called Amazon many times in my tall life. It sucks. But I had to realize that even if what they said were true, it couldn't truly hurt me.

> **A man's wisdom gives him patience; it is to his glory to overlook an offense.**
>
> **—King Solomon***

1. *Don't let her see you sweat.* Just like other Mean Girl tactics, name-calling is used to make you mad. So the number one thing you have to remember is, *don't let her see you sweat.* Don't react, or at least react totally differently than she expects you to. When you get hurt and retaliate, she wins, plain and simple. So hold your tongue unless you have something nice or funny to say. For example, I knew a girl who had really bad buckteeth that didn't even fit in her mouth. One time a girl called her a vampire and then looked at her friends and giggled. The bucktoothed girl looked at them, smiled, and said, "I know, and when I go like this, I look just like a bunny rabbit." She lifted her upper lip and made a rabbit face. The girls didn't know what to do. It totally took them off guard. They had slammed her, but she totally didn't mind; in fact, she made a joke of it. After a couple of seconds

**from the book of Proverbs chapter 19, verse 11

they all started laughing, and she went on her way. They don't talk about her teeth anymore.

2. **Don't make yourself a victim.** Unfortunately, sometimes name-calling can turn into labeling. You might be called a geek, and then it just sticks. Again, don't sweat your cookies. Take it in stride. Remember, Microsoft guru Bill Gates is a geek, and he's one of the richest and most famous men in the world. Don't let the label you get ruin who you are. If it's true, then live it up. **Change it into something positive.** And if it's not true, then start the anti-label campaign. Prove them wrong by being who you *really* are, not who they are trying to make you.

Don't allow someone to make you a victim of their tongue.* If you do, you're allowing someone to be a force of negative change in your life. Remember, no matter what people call you, they can't change who you are. Only you and Christ can do that. If you choose to let others make you into their image, you lose—and you deny Christ, because he calls you to be made into his image, to *"put on the new self, which is being renewed in knowledge **in the image of its Creator"*** (the apostle Paul's letter to the Colossians, chapter 3, verse 10). Christ died to set you free—free from the enemy, free from yourself, and free from the Mean Girl. You might not be feeling it right now, but it's true: You are a child of a king, not the punch line of a bad joke. Don't let anyone convince you by the mean things they say that you are less than a princess. If you want to know how to turn it around and be the girl you were made to be, find out what pleases your Father. Find out how he wants you to react.

You live in a hurting world, one that has a ton of girls in it who hurt so bad that the only way they see to ease their pain is to put *others* in more pain. But you aren't like that. Your pain has hope. Your pain has release. When you get tired of being the butt of their jokes, remember this: *"Blessed is the man who perseveres under trial, because when he has stood the test, he will receive the crown of life that God has promised to those who love him"* (the book of James, chapter 1, verse 12).

The Revengers

If you are a girl and you live on this planet, you have probably had another girl try to get revenge on you. You did something either accidentally or on purpose that she didn't like, and she went after you. Revenge seems to be as essential to the female as shoes. Most girls operate by the saying, "Don't get mad, get even." After all, people think, if there is no God and no one who is looking out for you and protecting you, then you have to take control yourself. But we are different. With a belief in God, we don't have to get revenge, because it isn't our gig, it's God's. And what a relief. Trouble is that most girls don't get this, so they are going to forever be after other girls to get revenge.

But he said to me, "My grace is sufficient for you, for my power is made perfect in weakness." Therefore I will **boast** all the more gladly **about my weaknesses**, so that Christ's power may rest on me. That is why, for Christ's sake, **I delight** in weaknesses, in **insults**, in **hardships**, in **persecutions**, in **difficulties**. For **when I am weak, then I am strong**.

—Paul's 2nd letter to the Corinthians, chapter 12, verses 9 and 10

Check out *No Offense* on page 96, and *Stand Up to the Mean Girl* on page 108.

The best way to avoid revenge is to stop the cycle. You can't stop her from attacking you, but you don't have to fight back the same way. Here are 3 keys to ending revenge.

1. Don't retaliate. You don't need to get revenge for her revenge. Her anger is hers; don't let her infect you with it. Remember, she's the one suffering because she's the one who hurts so bad that she feels a need to hurt you back. You don't have to feel that way because you know that God works all things together for the good of those who love him (Romans 8:28). So don't say anything mean back, and don't do anything to get revenge. Just laugh it off, or at least hide your hurt until you're alone. You'll kill the anger and the cycle right there. If you don't believe me and do decide to get revenge, then all bets are off, and the war is on. Getting revenge only makes things worse, not better, so lay off!

2. Don't tell. If you run off and tell a teacher or someone in authority, you run the risk of keeping the revenge cycle going. Your Mean Girl will think she has to get you back for telling, and the cycle keeps on spinning. So if she hasn't threatened your life or hurt you physically, try to lay low.

3. Pray. This might sound totally trite because you've heard it so much, but you need to learn it now. Pray for her. God calls us to pray for our enemies (the Gospel of Matthew 5:44). This does two things: It gets our minds off ourselves, and it gets God on the case.

Check out more on how to stop the cycle in *The Mean Girl Cycle*, page 80.

The infamous 3-way call. Have you had it done to you? Your friend calls you and nonchalantly asks you about another friend or a guy. And after you spill your guts, you hear another person on the line who was listening in the entire time. Argh! Horrible for you. But for the other 2 it's juicy—the best way to find out what someone *really* thinks. Trouble is, it's an invasion of privacy and a way to royally screw up your relationships. Like you read in the book *Dateable,* if someone will do something for you, they'll do it to you. In other words, if someone will 3-way call *for you,* they'll 3-way call *on you* just as fast.

Mean Girls dig the 3-way call because it's a power trip. They can gather much-needed information *and* embarrass you to death, and all in a matter of 5 minutes.

Your best defense against a 3-way call?

1. Shut up. Don't ever, and I mean *ever,* say anything about anyone that you wouldn't want them to hear you say. Yes, 3-way calling, as terrible as it is, might actually be a way to get you to start talking the way God would have you talk. You've heard the saying, "If you don't have anything good to say, then don't say anything at all." It's not a cliché for no reason—it's true. So shut up. If you want to avoid 3-way call trauma, then never, I mean *never,* say anything mean about anyone, to anyone. Then they can't trick you on a 3-way, and they will never be able to get you with their meanness.

2. Don't do it. Don't go whining about girls 3-way calling if you are doing the same thing to other girls! Remember, you are going to be judged for the same thing you are getting all sassy about—or haven't you heard? *"Why worry about a speck in your friend's eye when you have a log in your own? How can you think of saying, 'Let me help you get rid of that speck in your eye,' when you can't see past the log in*

your own eye? Hypocrite! First get rid of the log from your own eye; then perhaps you will see well enough to deal with the speck in your friend's eye" (Matthew 7:3–5 NLT).

So don't do it. Never, ever 3-way call someone in secret! It's just not cool. What it really says is that you are so completely wrapped up in what someone thinks of you that you have to find out if whatever it is *you* think *they* think is true. Bad, bad, bad. I wouldn't want to be you when God passes judgment. He's really not too keen on you seeking to get the approval of men over him. (Check it out: Pick up the book of Galatians and read chapter 1, verse 10.)

Slammers and Other Haters

A lot of girls aren't content to hate you themselves—they want everyone else to hate you too, or at least to say they do. The slam letter or other cruel stuff they might write in their blog* and the like are evil and angry attempts to rise above you by bringing you down way low. Mean Girls want to make you mad, and who wouldn't be mad if the entire class signed a notebook saying they hated you? It's cruel and unusual punishment. If you are the victim of a slam campaign, then you are the victim of a Really Mean Girl.

What do you do?

1. **Find your hope in your God.** This slam is probably the worst thing another girl could do to you, and she has no right. But I can't give you a magical way to get through it. The only thing you can do is cling to the Father. He promises that if you do, you will see the other side. *"I have told you these things, so that in me you may have peace. In this world you will have trouble. But take heart! I have overcome the world"* (Jesus, quoted in John chapter 16, verse 33). You

*For those of you who live under a rock and don't know what blogging is, it's online journaling. Some nasty little girls like to slam other girls on their blog just to make life miserable for them.

30

are always on God's mind, even in the midst of this. Ask yourself, *Where is my hope? What is God doing in this? How can I use this trial to draw closer to him?* You can draw closer by relying on him to use stuff like this to make you more holy, by reading more Scripture, and by praying more. Will this horrible thing done to you speed you into his arms? Some of the most amazing spiritual experiences and advances in my life have come from terrible grief. I've learned to lean into the pain instead of fearing it. I used to think, "I can't bear it. I will surely die," but then I realized that pain can't kill you, so I decided to lean into it like a bull rider leans into the bull. And on the other side I found glory.

"In this you greatly rejoice, though now for a little while you may have had to suffer grief in all kinds of trials. These have come so that your faith—of greater worth than gold, which perishes even though refined by fire—may be proved genuine and may result in praise, glory and honor when Jesus Christ is revealed" (the 1st letter from Peter, chapter 1, verses 6–7).

2. **Don't get mad.** The Mean Girl's goal is to make you mad, so when you react in anger, she wins. So what if you don't react in anger? How many points does she get? Zero!

3. **Don't get sad.** Another point for her is when she makes you sad. And if you cry, that's major pointage to her side. So if you don't react, then how many points does she get? Zero. And if you react the opposite of what the slam letter says—for example, if it says you are a mean slut but you react by being nice and kind to everyone—*you* actually get points. So think about this like a game or a battle. You have to think of it logically and not emotionally, or you will lose. And the more you lose, the more she comes after you, because she's lazy and she loves an easy win.

4. **Ignore 'em.** Mean people hate to be ignored. They hate it when their precious attack goes unnoticed. So do all you can to ignore her, even if it means holding on with all you've got till you get home and you can vent.

5. **Confront carefully.** Ignoring is usually best, but if you feel sure that God is telling you to confront the girl, never do it in front of her friends. She will be trying to impress them, and you'll never get through to her. And don't do it on the phone or on IM, because you don't know who she might be with. Find a place where you can be alone, like the library or at her house. Before you say anything, spend time figuring out how to say it in love. You have every right to speak for yourself, just be sure you speak in love and peace and don't corner her. You might try to ask her what you have done to make her hate you. When she tells you, don't argue with her. Remember, this isn't about flesh and blood but the spirit world. What is the enemy trying to do through this?

6. **Know when to tell.** You have to judge the degree of mean to decide what you should do about it. If the slam binder or blog or whatever it is starts threatening violence, then you have to tell. But if it's not something that scares you, then don't tell, because telling unnecessarily will only add fuel to the fire and keep the cycle going. Remember, when Mean Girls get bored, they often give up. Don't be their entertainment, and they will get tired of bothering you.

Unfortunately, some girls might never give up. You might have to put up with her hatred as long as you are in the same school together. Check out *Standing Up to the Mean Girl* (page 108) to find ways to stay strong.

Some Mean Girls are too wimpy to attack you in person, so they resort to cyberspace.* Maybe you've gotten a nasty text message on your cell or an IM that insulted your clothes or your body. In some freaky cases embarrassing pictures or videos are circulating. What would you do if you were this real-life kid? A 15-year-old (who here shall remain nameless) videotaped himself acting out a scene from *Star Wars* with a golf ball retriever as his light saber. Soon some other kids got ahold of the video, doctored it up with music from *The Matrix* and *Chicago,* and put it on the Internet. Now this kid is the most downloaded guy of the year. Utter embarrassment! What would you do if something like that happened to you? Would you drop out of school? Go loopy on us? How would you handle it? How would God have you handle it? Check out these two scenarios and decide which one you think is victorious and faithful:

> "It is God's business, not ours, to care for what we have. God is able to protect what we possess. We can trust him [with our things and our relationships]. The lock on the door is not what protects the house. Simplicity means the freedom to trust God for these and all things."
>
> **—Richard Foster**

Option 1. You freak out so much you change schools so you don't have to be seen again by anyone who saw you on video. But the next school you go to has seen you already too. It's all over the Internet. So you drop out again, and your mom homeschools you while you go to a counselor to ease the pain. Now you're all alone and the laughingstock of your city, maybe even the world. Did you win?

Option 2. You go to school and ask the teacher if you can talk to the class. She says yes, and you give the best Oscar acceptance speech anyone could ever give. You show a clip of your video and point out all the subtleties of your geekiness. The

*1 in 17 kids ages 10 to 17 had been threatened or harassed online.

class goes crazy with laughter as you smile and say, "Thanks for making me the most downloaded girl in America! And thanks to the Academy!"

Instantly you're the most popular girl in school. Everyone loves funny people, and you just took an embarrassment and made it a joke. Remember, if you make fun of yourself, you take away the power of the slam from the other person.

In the movie *8 Mile*, Rabbit, the character played by rapper Eminem, is in a rapping contest where the goal is to slam the other contestant in front of the roaring crowd. I'll save you the experience of sitting through the language, raunchy content, and bad acting by describing this particular scene. When Rabbit's life hits its most humiliating depths, he is sure to lose. But knowing his competitor will make fun of his failures and embarrassments, Rabbit turns the tables and raps with all his might about his miserable life. He points out all the bad things that have happened to him. He mocks himself and makes jokes, and by the end of his rap, his opponent has nothing left to make fun of because Rabbit did it all himself. If you feel this desperate, then you might want to consider throwing in the towel and joining the crowd. If you can make it a joke that you are in on, you can use a humiliating moment as an upper instead of a downer. It's called "stealing their thunder."

Unlike Rabbit's situation, it's physically impossible for you to go nose to nose with your Mean Girl in cyberspace. So what do you do? If you want to avoid, get away from, or "Rabbitize" cyber-attacks, here are some things to consider.

1. *Ignore them.* When you are on the Internet, act the same as in person. Ignore them. Don't argue back with the Mean Girl. Just hit delete or close. If you get an email from someone you don't know or trust, don't read it. Just delete it.

2. *Get off the Internet.* If you know a Mean Girl has a blog, what are you doing going to her site to read it? If

you're getting cyber-slammed, take a break and unplug. Start to spend less time on the Internet and more time with friends and family. Read a book; play with the dog. The more time you spend glued to the Net, the more chances for cyber-attack.

3. Beware. You never know if the person IMing or emailing you is really who they say they are. It could be someone pretending to be someone else. And don't believe everything you read or see on the Internet. If you are naive you can be taken for a ride. Be smart. I'll say it again: Don't trust everything you read.

4. Hang up the phone. I know it seems impossible, but turn your cell off. Don't have it on all day for text messaging. If you aren't available for harassing, then they are less likely to harass you.

5. Laugh. Remember not to take yourself too seriously. If people are circulating photos or videos of you, remember to laugh with them. See if their blog or website allows you to post comments. Be funny and pull a "Rabbit" out of your hat by posting an even crazier picture of yourself. If you or someone you know has the skills, make your own blog and get creative. Lighten up. When you take yourself and them too seriously, you make a bigger mess of a little thing that you might not even remember 10 years from now. (Read *So Offended*, page 96.)

For more info on what to do with a cyber-Mean Girl, check out www.meangirls.net.

"You're So Skinny!" and Other Insults

My Big Fat Obnoxious Compliment

Girls compete with each other about who is fattest. You know it's true; heck, you've done it. "I'm so fat today," your friend says. And to ease her troubled mind, you say, "Well, at least you aren't as fat as me!" Or a girl says, "I hate it, you are so skinny!" and you say, "Oh, no, I'm totally bloated." You grasp at anything to point out that you indeed are not skinny but fat. How sweet of you, and oh how self-degrading. But let me ask, why do you think that being the fattest makes you better? Why do we as girls think that to be skinny is an insult to the other girl, so much so that we have to quickly deny any connection whatsoever to skinny?

It's a strange phenomenon that I've noticed in my journey, this condition peculiar to girls—you just don't hear guys arguing over who's fattest. Somehow cutting yourself down is the only acceptable response to a compliment in girl world. It's as if a compliment is a hot potato or a flaming arrow that has to be dodged and denied. And it isn't just about weight. Remember a girl telling you, "I love that outfit," and your response of "Oh, this old thing? It's all I could find to put on today, and I feel totally hideous." Or try saying, "I'm really bad at math," and watch another girl say something like, "At least you're better at it than me." It's always the same. Deflect the compliment by slamming yourself.

In girl world the compliment is an interesting tactic of dissection. It serves as a precision cutting instrument in the hands of a conniving girl. In our discussion of why girls are mean, the compliment phenomenon is a very useful one to understand.

When you get a compliment from a girl, your immediate response is probably to deny it. That's because you assume that now that she's pointed out a good thing about you, she must be feeling inferior. So to keep her from feeling inferior, you choose to degrade yourself by denying the compliment to save her from feeling any worse about herself and getting downright mean because of it. Add on something that cuts yourself down, and *BAM*, you've just gifted the giver with a beautiful package of your own.

It's a natural female urge to protect the feelings of others and to keep them from hating you. We are born to care for others, not to destroy them, so our natural response to a potential hurt feeling is to scramble to the rescue. Many a researcher might say that girls tend to deny compliments and turn them to self-degradation because of low self-esteem. And to that I say, pooey. There might be a smidge of bad body image in the degradation, but for the most part it's self-protection. I believe when you deny a compliment, your main goal is to protect the feelings of the giver and thus save yourself from creating another enemy. In other words, the girl has thrown out an insecurity, something that she's potentially jealous of, and your job is to make her feel secure again.

> When you deny a compliment, your main goal is to protect the feelings of the giver and thus save yourself from creating another enemy.

The trouble is that your mind is simple. It believes whatever it reads, sees, or hears most, especially from you. And so if you continue to tell others your faults in order to make them feel good about themselves, you continue to reinforce in your mind a negative self-image. And *that's* when the research proves true. It's a self-fulfilling prophecy. Imagine if I were to tell myself every morning as I lay in bed,

I hate mornings.
I hate getting up.
I'm not a morning person.
I just hate mornings.

I would find it very, very hard to get up. Why? Well, maybe it's true that I'm more of a night person, but the truth is that I've just made it worse by training my brain to think that it not only loves the nights but *hates* the mornings. But you could choose to stop this negative input and replace it with something more positive and true, like,

I can get a lot of stuff done in the mornings.
I have the ability to get up early.
Getting up early isn't as hard as I thought.

Then you would find that getting up can get easier. This is why Paul wrote to the Philippians,

> Finally, brothers, whatever is true, whatever is noble, whatever is right, whatever is pure, whatever is lovely, whatever is admirable—if anything is excellent or praiseworthy—think about such things. Whatever you have learned or received or heard from me, or seen in me—put it into practice. And the God of peace will be with you.
>
> Philippians chapter 4, verses 8–9

God created us so that thinking good, honest, and godly thoughts brings you peace. Researchers even found the power of this positive thinking when they studied athletes. They gave the same workout routine to 2 groups of bicyclists. They all had to ride 5 miles a day around the city. Half of that time they spent riding up hills and the other half down hills. One group was taken aside and told that they were to think for at least 10 minutes a day about how much they hate riding up hills. The other was told that they were to tell themselves for at least 10 minutes a day what a great workout they got riding up hills. At the end of a week, they compared the two groups' riding times. The first group, those who told themselves that they hated hills, had considerably worse times than the other group. They said that when they got to the hills, they just lost energy. Their minds learned what they told them and acted upon it.

Your mind is listening to everything you tell it. So be careful about what you say, or you will create a monster. Tell yourself every day that you are fat and watch your mind try to make sure that's true. Your mind has to think it's right. If it hears that you are fat over and over, then it becomes convinced that you are fat regardless of the real truth. That's why anorexics see themselves as fat when we all see them as thin. The mind believes what we repeatedly think and say. Think about what you want your mind to do and to create. Think about it very carefully next time you want to respond to a compliment in a self-degrading way. Is that really who you want to make yourself to be? If not, then zip it. Don't say anything but thank you.

Mean Uses of the Compliment/Slam Technique

The Combo. *"You are so skinny, I hate you."* Is it a compliment? Is it a slam? This one delivered with just the right sweet tone is a slam in compliment's clothing. How could anyone get mad after receiving a compliment? So what if there is an angry message attached to it? You can't deny that the compliment was there, so you immediately look for a way to degrade yourself to make the giver of this double-edged compliment feel better. What a great delivery of an evil cut—she makes you feel bad for her after she has slammed you. It's ingenious, really.

So what do you do with this combo? How do you react? Just like you do with every other slam: smile and move along. A lot of girls might not realize that this combo can be hurtful, so give them the benefit of the doubt and trust that they mean well. But as you practice to control your own mean streak, stay away from the compliment/slam combo. If you want to compliment someone, don't tack on a hateful comment. It isn't necessary or complimentary. Remember, girls are afraid of ticking other girls off, so don't give them cause to fear. It just isn't cool!

The Hidden Slam. *"I love that dress."* Sounds simple enough, but we all know that it's not *what you say* but *how you say it* and what you really mean that counts. Either way, with the hidden slam compliment, you have to take it with a smile. If you fight back or act snotty in return, you lose. I repeat: You lose. She gets a point by making you mad. So even though the compliment she just threw at you wasn't meant as a compliment, just smile sweetly and move along. Heck, you might even throw in a "thank you" and a smile. Do all you can to take it as a compliment and move on.

If it is totally obvious that she is being mean and doesn't have an ounce of sincerity—i.e., if she is with a group of girls and they all giggle as she says it—you can *still* just smile knowingly and keep on moving. There's no use saying anything mean in return. It will only make matters worse. Her presence is merely a bleep on the radar, nothing more. She doesn't rock your world or impact it in any way, so don't let her. Don't make it more than what it is, a catty little comment. In 10 years it won't mean a thing. (Besides, you don't always know people's intentions. She might actually be being nice, so always react gracefully, and you always win. You won't get framed as a Mean Girl by attacking a compliment. Bad move.)

And if you are a big fan of the hidden slam, shame on you. Your job in life isn't to destroy people but to build them up. If you are bent on destroying others, know that God is watching and he isn't pleased. So avoid the hidden slam. It doesn't do anybody any good, and it isn't funny.

See *The Mean Girl Cycle* on page 80 and *Getting Even Is Getting Mean* on page 86 for more on this.

The best way to handle a compliment is to accept it and give it back. Simply say thank you and then give a compliment back. Warning: Girls are often afraid of a confident girl, so be prepared—when you say thank you, they might be shocked, but complimenting them back will soothe their shock a bit. It's hard being a confident girl. It can leave you open as a target because the Mean Girl will feel insecure with you around. But stand your ground. Just because she is defective doesn't mean you have to be as well.

Check out *Changing a Mean Girl*, page 93.

Why Is the Mean Girl in Your Life?

"Why me, God?" I used to ask. *"Why do these girls hate me so much?"* I struggled with that issue for years, long after school was over and done with. When I started working I found out girls were just as bad there as in school. Conniving, backstabbing, and manipulative, only this time they had power over me. Unfortunately, big girls can be just as mean as younger girls. You think they will go away or just get better, but they never do. So why do Mean Girls exist? What is God's reason for allowing them in our lives? After all, nothing happens without his okay. He's the boss, the real boss. So what's up with Mean Girls? *"Why, God, why?"*

"Why not?" might be his response. Why are you so surprised when bad things happen to you, as if the world were outside of the control of the power of darkness? (Read 1 Peter 4:12 and 1 John 5:19–20.) Why are you asking God *why* instead of asking *what* you should do in response? After all, is he a God who should be questioned (Isaiah 45:11)? Why not rather ask him, "What am *I* doing that might cause this reaction to me?"

As you read through this book, you will find things you can do that might help you ease the pain caused by the Mean Girl and might even ease her pain. But before you get to that, you have to realize that the most important thing is how *you* react to *her*, not how much *she* changes. How will you prove your perseverance if you have nothing to persevere through? How will you learn to love your enemies if you have no enemies? Before we go any further, you have to consider who you want to be and what you want your reaction to the Mean Girl to look like. If you believe every word in the Bible is true, then you will find that you have only one choice. Scripture clearly states that your goal as a believer is to please God, not man (Galatians 1:10), and, surprise, not even yourself. "For even Christ did not please himself" (Romans 15:3). So why does God allow you to face a Mean Girl?

See *God's Plan for Your Mean Girl* on page 115.

One of the big reasons God allows trials and junk in our lives is to purify us. It's like that refiner's fire everyone always talks about—the fire that burns off all the impurities and keeps all the good parts of the metal. You have to be purified, and purification takes place in extreme ways, like fires (1 Peter 1:7) and Mean Girls. So if she is your refiner's fire, what will your reaction be? Will you fight against your refining, or will you turn to God and say, "What shall I become for you?" If you can learn to act the way God calls you to act in the face of the Mean Girl, then you will get closer and closer to being who he called you to be.

Look at it like this:

1. Does it feel like the Mean Girl in your life is a trial, a challenge?   **Yes   No**
2. Does she cause you grief?   **Yes   No**
3. Does she wear on your patience?   **Yes   No**
4. Does she test your ability to "turn the other cheek" to your enemy (Luke 6:29)?   **Yes   No**

If you answered yes to any of these, let's look deeper into God's Word to find out why she is in your life.

Trials and the Mean Girl
What does God have to say about it?

"Consider it pure joy, my sisters whenever you face **Mean Girls** of many kinds, because you know that the testing of your faith by a **Mean Girl** develops perseverance. Perseverance must finish its work so that you may be mature and complete, not lacking anything."

paraphrase of the book of James,
the first chapter, verses 2–4

According to this paraphrased verse, what exactly do
    Mean Girls do?
What things highlighted in the verse do you want?

When it comes to all the junk she pulls:

> In this you greatly rejoice, though now for a little while you may
> have had to suffer grief in all kinds of trials *with all kinds of
> mean girls*. These *mean girls* have come so that your faith—of
> greater worth than gold, which perishes even though refined by
> fire—may be proved genuine and may result in praise, glory and
> honor when Jesus Christ is revealed.
>
> book of 1 Peter, chapter 1, verses 6–7, paraphrased

Why have these Mean Girls come into your life, accord-
    ing to this verse?
Does that look like a good thing?   Yes   No

The Mean Girl in your life is not punishment from God. She
might not have even been sent by God, but he is going to use
her to purify your faith. Remember, he uses all things together
for the good of the people who love him (Romans 8:28). He uses
'em all, Mean Girls and all, for your good, if you allow it. But if
you decide to take this problem and fix it yourself by getting even
or mad, then you blew any proving or testing you were going
through. You flunked. You didn't pass. No refining. And when
you fail a class, what happens? Yep, Repeatsville! You have to
take it over again. So you didn't pass the test the first time and
what do you know if *she* doesn't come back again, right at ya.
See, if you don't handle trials the way God tells you to—quietly,
patiently, lovingly—then you'll start to notice a funny thing:
They might just keep repeating till you get them right, whether
it's the same girl or a different Mean Girl.

"*Great,*" you say. "So I've failed over and over. What am I supposed to do to get it right?" First of all, let me tell you that it's

okay that you failed. Failure just tells you what *not to do,* and that gets you one step closer to what *to* do. And remember, you are forgiven for failure. There is no condemnation when you are in Christ (see Romans 8:1), only forgiveness, so don't get all dragged down by thinking what a failure you are. That's not coming from God. He wants you to get on with your life and get over it. (If you aren't getting this, stop right now and look up these verses in a Bible: Romans 7:14–8:1; 1 John 1:9.) And remember, you don't have to feel forgiven to be forgiven. Don't judge your spiritual state based on how you feel but on what God's Word says. If you don't accept his forgiveness and move on, you are calling him a liar. His Word says you are forgiven (Acts 10:43; Ephesians 1:7), so you'd best believe his Word.

I hope now that you are starting to see that one of the reasons you have a Mean Girl in your life could be to test your faith and prove it pure. She might be just what you need in order to be purified. But wait, there's more.

▌ Dying to Self

Do you believe that God's will and plan is better than yours? Do you believe that what Jesus taught is holy and good for your spirit? If you do, then you will agree that his commands are good and therefore to be followed. So, I ask, how can you prove to him that you believe his words are good unless you have a mean person in your life to test you? Check it out:

> If someone strikes you on one cheek, turn to him the other also. If someone takes your cloak, do not stop him from taking your tunic. Give to everyone who asks you, and if anyone takes what belongs to you, do not demand it back. Do to others as you would have them do to you. **If you love those who love you, what credit is that to you?** Even "sinners" love those who love them. And if you do good to those who are good to you, what credit is that to you? Even "sinners" do that. And if you lend to those from whom you expect repayment, what credit is that to you? Even "sinners" lend

to "sinners," expecting to be repaid in full. **But love your enemies, do good to them, and lend to them without expecting to get anything back**. Then your reward will be great, and you will be sons of the Most High, because he is kind to the ungrateful and wicked. Be merciful, just as your Father is merciful.

Luke 6:29–36

If you had only nice people in your life, you could never prove your obedience to this verse. You need mean people, enemies, in order to prove that this verse is true in your life. If you just love the people who love you back, what good is that? How do you prove your ability to love and to follow God's rules if all you do is what is easy and natural to sinful man? You prove nothing. But when a Mean Girl comes into your life, you have the opportunity to prove your faith in and love for God. She is your chance to say, "Yes, God, I believe your Word is true, and I will work it into my life no matter what." She is your chance to shine, your chance to prove to yourself and to your God that his Word is more important than your ego.

Over 2000 years ago, Christ died on a cross. He died even though he didn't want to. He begged the Father to find another way (read the Gospel according to Mark, chapter 14, verse 36). But when there wasn't another way to take away your sins, he died willingly. And so now, some 2000 years later, he asks you to die to yourself. That old, sinful, me-protecting self—he asks you to die to that and to live for him. Don't believe me? Then how do you explain these words:

Then Jesus said to his disciples, "If anyone would come after me, he must deny himself and take up his cross and follow me."

Matthew 16:24

For you died, and your life is now hidden with Christ in God.

Colossians 3:3

> Those who belong to Christ Jesus have crucified the sinful nature with its passions and desires.
>
> Galatians 5:24

Your Mean Girl might just be your opportunity to die to self (see *Get Over Yourself,* page 99). Are you willing to take the challenge and truly die to self?

Before you go any further, consider these words and decide if you believe them. Because if you do, then you have only one choice:

> Slaves, **submit yourselves** to your masters with all respect, not only to those who are good and considerate, but also **to those who are harsh. For it is commendable if a man bears up under the pain of unjust suffering because he is conscious of God.** But how is it to your credit if you receive a beating for doing wrong and endure it? But **if you suffer for doing good and you endure it, this is commendable** before God. To this you were called, because **Christ suffered for you, leaving you an example,** that you should follow in his steps. "He committed no sin, and no deceit was found in his mouth." **When they hurled their insults at him, he did not retaliate; when he suffered, he made no threats.** Instead, he entrusted himself to him who judges justly.
>
> 1 Peter 2:18–23

Every believer's goal should be to become more and more like Christ. In this part of God's Word, we see that this task means suffering through Mean Girls without retaliation or threats. I know it hurts to have a Mean Girl in your life, but **God never asked you to respond to your feelings;** he only asks you to obey his Word. His commands never have to do with ordering you to feel good about doing things; they are just to do them. Feelings can't be commanded. Right now I can't tell you "Feel happy!" and expect you to do it. Feelings aren't something that can be commanded to be turned on. So don't ever expect God to command you to feel better but rather expect him to command you to *act* better.

A funny thing happens when you act according to God's Word: You will soon find that good feelings follow. If you make it your number one goal to act according to God's commands, I promise you that better feelings will soon follow. Yet dying to self isn't an exercise in joy or even peace; it is simply a believer's obedience to a command from their Father. If you live to please God, you will find that following his commands is the only option for your Mean Girl problem.

■ Your Creation

The final proposal I have for the reason for your Mean Girl might come as a shock. This one might not apply to you, and if it does, you might not want to believe me. But think about it honestly: Sometimes a Mean Girl is your own creation.

A lot of times girls are mean to you because of what you've done either knowingly or unknowingly. I have had times in my life when I really didn't trust girls. And so I retreated to the world of boys. I spent all my time with them and cut off any contact with girls. As I look back now, I see that it might have made me a few enemies, because what I was showing, subconsciously, was that I didn't like girls. I was passing judgment on them, and who likes to be judged? The way I behaved by avoiding them altogether might have been the very thing that drove them to hate me. So you see, I could have in fact created my own Mean Girls by the way I acted around girls. You might have created your own Mean Girl in other ways. Like maybe you are too sensitive and are always on the defensive when girls talk to you. That makes you a dangerous girl, because they never know when you will blow up, and girls tend to be mean to dangerous girls—it's their faulty self-protection mode.

See *Why Are You So Easy to Hate?* on page 75.

I hate to even say this, but it might be true, and we have to consider all angles: You might be a Mean Girl yourself, without even knowing it. You've gossiped about someone, hurt their feelings, and now they are after you. You've lied about her and now she's getting you back. Or maybe you just judged her for not being a good girl, so she's after you now. She could be mad at you for any number of reasons, and a lot of them could be something you have done yourself.

So as you read this book I want you to be totally honest with yourself. If you want to get rid of the Mean Girl in your life, you have to analyze your life. You have to be honest and really assess how you live, what you do, and how you do it. If there are Mean Girls in your life because of something you are doing, then congratulations, that means you have the power to change things. You are actually in a better position than the girl who honestly isn't doing anything to provoke her, because in your case you can do something concrete to change your life today.

Listen, even if a lightbulb is going off over your head right now about something you might be doing to make her mad, I want you to understand that changing it today won't make things all better tomorrow. If you've done something mean that has sent her on a rampage, mending fences might take time. But with apologies and forgiveness, over time you *can* fix the mess you've made. So don't start freaking out about this; just keep it in the back of your mind that if your goal is to get rid of your Mean Girl, then you might have to start with yourself. You might not think you have an ounce of mean in you, but I believe that if we are honest, we will all find some bit of mean that can be cleaned up. And with that cleaned up, you might find a world of nice girls open up to you like you've never seen before. So be ready to be honest as you keep reading this book. Be ready to analyze yourself and those girls around you, and by the end you should be ready to take on all the Mean Girls in your life just the way your God wants you to.

Mean Girl behind Bars

Mean Starts in Your Mind

In January of 1995, 18-year-old Christa Pike got really jealous of a 19-year-old girl who liked her boyfriend. So Christa convinced her boyfriend that the girl had to be taken care of. And by "taken care of" she meant destroyed. So on January 12, 1995, Christa and her boyfriend took the girl to a park and tortured her for 30 minutes. They mutilated her with a box cutter, smashed her skull with asphalt, and took a jagged piece as a souvenir.

After the brutal murder Christa went back home and bragged to her friends about her bloody attack. To her it was justified: The girl was making her life miserable, so she had a right to get her back.

This kind of thing seems unbelievably violent and cruel. It's stuff from the headlines and horror films, but it's real, and it's the result of a lie that one girl told herself. And that lie is that she deserves to get even. She believed she had the power to destroy another person in order to make herself happier, so she used it. But it backfired on this girl, who now sits on death row in Tennessee, awaiting her execution. She spends 23 to 24 hours a day locked in her cell, feeling alone, abandoned, and empty. I wonder if she now thinks it was worth it to get rid of that pesky competitor for her boyfriend's attention.

In Matthew 5:28 Jesus says that if you even look at someone with lust in your eyes, it's as if you've slept with them. You don't have to actually do what you are thinking for it to have ramifications. If what he says is true (and I believe it is), we can assume that whatever you think has results that are far bigger than just thinking and in fact are the same as doing. Think about sleeping with someone, and it's like you already have.

If you have a sudden thought of sleeping with someone but you quickly clear that out of your mind, then that's just temptation, not sin. It's not like daydreaming about it or thinking about it for a longer time than the second it entered your mind. But sitting and pondering a sexual encounter with someone, thinking about it over and over, is simply the same thing as doing it. God reads your thoughts. He knows that sex show you have going. And surprise, surprise, he is in on the hate fest that you might have against someone too. So the next time you start to fantasize about doing something mean to someone, check yourself. It's no different to God than if you are actually doing it. It's all a sin. Bad, bad, bad.

The Bible is an amazing book, and the psychological understanding that it conveys is astounding. See, the more you think about something, the more likely you are to do it. Christa Pike certainly fantasized about killing that girl long before she actually did it. In his paraphrase of the book of James, Eugene Petersen writes, "The temptation to give in to evil comes from us and only us. We have no one to blame but the leering, seducing flare-up of our own lust. Lust gets pregnant, and has a baby: sin! Sin grows up to adulthood, and becomes a real killer" (chapter 1, verses 14–15, MESSAGE). So don't even start to plot or dream about how you will get even, 'cause your brain is an open book to your God. Will you be holy in thought as well as deed? You are held accountable for both.

Check out what Jesus said:

> But I say, if you are angry with someone, you are subject to **judgment**! If you call someone an idiot, you are in danger of being **brought before the high council**. And if you curse someone, you are in danger of the **fires of hell**.
>
> Matthew 5:22 NLT

Let's break it down by the results:

Judgment—You are subject to judgment if you are angry with someone. This is talking about the judgment of God. Yikes. Not anything to mess with, since he's all-powerful.

Brought before the high council—This refers to the heavenly high council, a high council like the one that sat on earth in Jesus' time, only this one is in heaven and passes judgment on everyone. Again, yikes. Not a good court to have to sit before. Worse than Judge Judy, Judge Wapner, and Judge Hatchett combined could ever be.

Fires of hell—Just what it sounds like. If you call someone a name or curse them, you risk sending yourself to hell.

Now, if you read more of what Jesus said and did, you find that you are forgiven for whatever you do if you believe in his saving power and make him Lord. But, my girls, if you think that you can choose to sin against God willfully, deliberately, and repeatedly and then escape any punishment or discipline, you are way off base (check out the book of Hebrews, chapter 12, verses 5–7).

So the next time you start to daydream about revenge on Little Miss Mean, think twice. Seriously, think two times: once to think "Stop this!" and once to replace that thought with something holy. Pray for her, pray for yourself, or whatever—just think twice.

Are You Doing Something Wrong?

Now, before we go on, I want to ask you a seriously hard question. You have to be completely honest with yourself right now, because if you aren't, then you could be dealing with Mean Girls the rest of your life. Here it is: Do they continue to call you the same thing no matter where you are? No matter what school you transfer to, no matter which group you are with, do they continually hate you for the same reasons?

Sometimes when the torture repeats itself no matter where you are, a pattern forms, and the only thing common to that pattern is you. Let's look at it logically: If you are the only thing that is the same in every situation, then something about you might be drawing the harassment, and you might need to see what it is. Now, in this exercise I don't want you to get all psycho on me and start blaming yourself for what's going on. That's a lie, and you shouldn't buy it. That's a pity party, and it's not faith. (Read the apostle Paul's letter to the Romans, chapter 8, verse 1.)

What you need to do is be truthful and honest with yourself. Is there something about you that causes girls to react to you a certain way? What is the repeated insult? Can you find any truth in it whatsoever? If so, then is that something you or your God wants you to change? If you are unsure, then find out. Think about the names and the gossip. What is the usual slam? Is it "Little Miss Goody-Two-Shoes"? If so, then check yourself—are you projecting your beliefs onto them, judging them for not being as pure as you are? If not, then why else would they be calling you that? Ask God to show you. Pick up your Bible and find out what he wants to tell you. Do a study on judging others and one on loving others. Do you complain a lot? Then don't expect people to want to be around you (see Philippians chapter 2, verse 14). Are you always scared of people who might try to bring you into their circle, distrusting that they could like you (see the book of Psalms, chapter 56, verses 3–4)? Then read *The Outsider* on page 55. What is God saying to you? It never hurts to be serious about understanding yourself and your interaction with others. If you get bad grades in every class you take, you can't blame it on bad teachers. They were all different teachers; you were the only one who was the same in all those classes. Don't lie to yourself about yourself; that's a weapon of the enemy. God asks you to be honest (Philippians chapter 4, verse 8). He wants you to know yourself and to realize that you become what you think about most often. "As [a man] thinketh in his heart so is he" (Proverbs 23:7 KJV).

This is serious stuff. All these Mean Girl experiences might just be a call for you to get real with yourself. Ask God to help you examine your heart. (Read how David did this in Psalm 139, verses 23–24.) What about you rubs other girls wrong? If you can honestly say nothing, then bravo! Well done, good and faithful servant of God. But if you think you might have room for improvement, dive on in and get to work. You will have girls in your life for the rest of your life. Why not learn to live in peace with them?

Why Does She Hate You?

No one has any right to hate you, but not having a right never stopped anybody. For centuries girls have hated other girls, and those girls have asked why. In the pages that follow, you will find out some of the warped reasons why your Mean Girl might hate you.

Your main goal is to get the Mean Girl to leave you alone. When you understand more about her, you might be able to find ways to distract her or even change her. The following list talks about the kinds of girls Mean Girls love to hate and what you can do if you are one of these girls.

The Outsider and Other Girls You Wouldn't Think Mean Girls Would Pick On

THE OUTSIDER

While speaking to a group of girls at a school, I was told the story of a girl who started going to the school and soon transferred. The girl who told the story smiled from the front row as she said, "This girl was just weird. No one could figure her out. I mean, we tried to be nice to her, but she just wasn't nice back. So one day we took her wallet from her and flushed it down the toilet. It was pretty funny. Then we just yelled at her whenever we saw her, 'Why won't you talk, freak girl?' And before you know it, she had to transfer to another school. She just couldn't handle the pressure." The storyteller looked around the room at all her friends and enemies and smiled triumphantly.

Our topic was Mean Girls, and she felt like that was the perfect story to tell us about Mean Girls—the Mean Girl being the one who had to transfer. "Why was she mean?" I asked. "Because she wouldn't talk to any of us," she said quickly, as if I were an idiot. "We're glad she's gone," she added.

In this little girl's world, it was all about her. Someone wasn't talking to *her,* so there must have been something wrong with that person. She didn't get the person, so there had to be a way to figure her out, to get her to be like "the rest of us," she justified.

Mean Girls aren't always mean on purpose, at least not in their minds. This little girl and her friends drove another girl to such pain that she had to move to be free from them, yet she saw no meanness in herself. The reason she didn't know she was being mean is that she was only thinking of herself and her own discomfort with a girl who didn't talk or act like her. She was oblivious to her own meanness until I confronted her with it. I'm still not sure she got it, since she was so absorbed in her own feelings, but we can hope that one day she will.

If you are the Outsider girl, you might like to learn more about why girls pick on you. Let's break it down to try to understand what the heck they are thinking. You haven't done anything wrong. You haven't done anything at all. All you've ever been is yourself. You might be different-looking; you might be quiet, or shy, or, well, just different. But you aren't mean. You aren't even involved. You stay out of their lives, so why can't they stay out of yours? Let's look at several reasons and see if you can find any that might fit your situation.

Reason #1: female bonding. It's a fact of life that girls bond when they can share juicy info about other people. It's like super glue that makes us best buds. In fact, it's hard to find best buds who don't, in some way or another, talk about other people. But an even stronger way of bonding is having a common enemy to talk about. Think about how Americans came together after the 9/11 attacks. Nothing else seemed important but getting our enemy. We were all obsessed with kicking some booty. Even Californians loved New York. That one enemy made us all lovey and supportive of each other. Same goes for girl world. If two girls have a common enemy, they feel really bonded.

Reason #2: *You're mean first.* This might be a total shock to you, but you might be starting the cycle of mean by reacting meanly to them in the first place. If you think girls are going to be mean to you, you might react bitterly even if they say something that isn't mean. It's because you *think* they are going to be mean. Remember that strange thing with the mind: You get whatever you think about most. If you think everyone is mean to you, they eventually will be because you are so hard to like when your defenses are up. Heck, they might just be scared of you because you come off so cranky.

So what can you do if you're the Outsider of choice for their meanness?

1. ## Don't be the easy enemy. Girls need something to bond around, and you, as the Outsider, are an easy target, an easy mark to become enemy number one. It's sad but true: Mean Girls are lazy, so they pick the easiest target they can find, and a loner is the easiest of all. It's like how when lions hunt they target the weakest animal of the herd, and it's usually the one that is separate from the others.

2. ## Lighten up your own attitude. If you're defensive, lighten up. Try not to react in anger no matter what they do. If you can muster the strength to just be nice, you might find out that they change their tune when it comes to you. You can't go your whole life thinking people are out to get you. If you do, then soon enough it becomes a self-fulfilling prophecy, and it happens only because it's what you planned for and reacted for. Expect more from people and you just might get it.

3. ## Stop the mean. Even if you aren't starting the mean cycle, you can still interrupt it and work for change in your own life by stopping the mean on your end. You have the

Read *Why Are You So Easy to Hate*, page 75, *No Offense*, page 96, and *God's Plan for Your Mean Girl*, page 115.

power to make a change in your heart and in your school by deciding you will not be mean back, no matter what. Read *The Mean Girl Cycle* on page 80 for more.

4. Learn to love. Okay, I know that sounds impossible. You don't love them. You are scared of them. I know, I know, but who's bigger here? Your God or your Mean Girl? He says to love her, so that's what you gotta do. But we'll start slow, okay? No death-defying feats. Here's what I want you to do from now on, and you can practice it on your family members if you need to:

a. **Look everyone in the eye** *when you approach them. It won't kill you, even though I know it will feel like it. But if you don't look into others' eyes, you can never love them.*

b. **Smile.** *Again, it won't kill you, but it might make you nauseous. You'll get over it, trust me. A smile is the best way to love on somebody. For some people it might be the only smile they get that day.*

c. **Go where the people are.** *Don't hide out. You were created to live in a community and to love others, not to be a hermit. That's hiding the love of God under a cup where no one can see it. He is more important than that. Don't worry about yourself; worry about him. Is he being seen in you, or are you hiding him from a world that desperately needs him?*

d. **Give people a break.** *They are all hurting just as much as you, believe it or not. Pray for them. Care for them. Show them you love them by noticing they exist. You aren't doing this for attention or for affection; you are doing this for God (see Galatians 1:10). So don't*

58

worry if they still make fun of you and don't get you. It will take time for them to adjust to your change. They haven't learned what you've learned, so they will need time to see you live it out over and over before they get the transformation. So don't fret.

Okay, so the Outsider is the easy target. She's all alone, usually a little defensive, and tons of fun to make squirm. But if that isn't you, then you are still scratching your head and saying, "Why are they picking on *me*?" Well, let's continue to explore.

Like I said earlier, Mean Girls are lazy. They go for the weakest link, the easiest target, but that's not always as obvious as the loner girl. Lots of times they pick on the most popular girl or the smartest girl. Or even the hottest girl. Why would they go after these kinds of girls? Ask me the same question and I'll tell you the same answer: because she's an easy target. Let's break it down.

THE POPULAR GIRL

You're popular; people like you. But still this girl or gaggle of girls just won't leave you alone. They are relentless in slamming you and trying to make you look bad. Whassup with that? Well, it's because of your popularity that you become an easy target. It's the same as on the outside (the outside of high school, that is). The most popular people have always and will always be slammed by others because it's easy. No one wants to hear bad things about Joe Schmo, but they sure love hearing bad stuff about Jennifer Aniston or Kate Hudson. It's human nature to want to hear bad stuff about people who are considered more successful than you. People like to see popular people, stars, and politicians in their worst possible light, because that takes the pain off of being not quite as popular.

See, if a girl who is less popular than you can slam you good, then she gets a point, and that ups her hip factor. And the reason she can attack you is because so many others like her are just as jealous of you as she is. So she knows right off she'll have an audience that will totally love what she has to say. Think about the *Globe* or the *Enquirer*, those papers you see at the checkout stand. They make tons of money off of unpopular (i.e., not famous) people who want to hear horror stories about the popular people (i.e., the famous ones). It's an industry. People will pay tons just to find out the latest trash, and it's no different at school, only what they pay is loyalty and friendship, not $1.95.

So don't be shocked if you are the target just because you are popular. It's the law of the jungle. But what do you do if you are popular and a target of a Mean Girl?

1. **Invite her.** Most of the time people pick on the popular girl because they are jealous. They feel unloved, left out, bitter. They are just hurt, and not really from anything you've done but from the thoughts that torture their own mind. So if you will learn to care about them, to take note of them, and to invite them into your circle, you will gain 2 benefits:

    a. *You will be obedient to God, who says that you are to love your enemies and your neighbor as yourself. "But I say, love your enemies! Pray for those who persecute you!" (the Gospel of Matthew, chapter 5, verse 44 NLT).*

    b. *You might just see a change in their behavior. It's really hard to be mean to someone who is nice to you all the time. Try this out on someone that isn't as scary. Next time you are at a restaurant or someplace where you are being helped by an unhappy or cranky person, say something nice to them. Compliment their necklace or tell them they have a nice smile. Say something that will make them show you that smile. A kind word can change a person's day and make them change their tune as well.*

So practice it next time you get a chance, and then go for it with the Mean Girl. Give her a nice card. Invite her to the movies. Save her a seat. I know this totally goes against what you want to do and what you feel is right, but oftentimes the right thing feels totally wrong. A lot of times the right thing goes against everything you've ever been taught, but check it out and see if it doesn't work. Or at least check it out in Scripture and see if it doesn't pay off.

- *Abraham was told to sacrifice Isaac, his only son—it felt totally wrong, but obeying God turned out to be totally right (see the book of Genesis, chapter 22).*
- *Noah was told to build an ark. Why? It had never flooded. It seemed totally illogical, but he followed God's command and saved his family (the book of Genesis, chapters 6 and 7).*
- *Jesus allowed himself to be hung on a cross. It was completely horrific and unimaginable, and he begged his Father for another way, but doing it was the right thing (the book of Luke, chapter 22, verse 42).*

2. **Talk her up.** You've heard the expression "kill 'em with kindness." Well, now's your chance. An ancient proverb says, "If your enemies are hungry, give them food to eat. If they are thirsty, give them water to drink. You will heap burning coals on their heads, and the LORD will reward you" (Proverbs chapter 25, verses 21–22 NLT). Now I know it looks like this proverb is telling you to burn your enemy, but dig a little deeper and you'll see that's not anywhere near the truth. In the days when this truth was written, people needed coals in order to keep their homes warm. If you were to give your enemy burning coals, then you would be warming them. You would be paying their heat-

ing bill. But why on the head? Well, you ever watch the Discovery Channel or read *National Geographic* and see those natives carrying sacks of rice, pots of water, and other heavy things on their heads? That is the way that many cultures carry things in the part of the world this came from. So one possible explanation for this verse has to do with helping your enemy by giving them fuel for their furnace. But there is another explanation for this verse, and it makes just as much sense; in fact, it's like a one-two punch. The Egyptians had a tradition in the days when this was written that when someone was guilty, they would pile burning coals in a pan on their head and walk through town as a sign of repentance for what they had done. So the one-two punch of being nice to your enemy is that 1) it's what you are called to do, and 2) it might actually lead them to saying they are sorry and to stopping the behavior, which is repentance. So with kindness you love your enemy, but you also help them to see the error in their ways.

I know what you're thinking: What an odd thing to do to your enemy—supply their needs, care for them? Seems preposterous! But again, illogical things are sometimes the most logical when you really look at them. Do something nice for your enemy, and they are no longer your enemy but your friend. It's hard to hate someone you are helping, and it's also hard for that person to hate you. This goes against everything the world has thrown at you, I know. But listen, the way the world has been doing it hasn't been working, so why would you want to copy the world? It's proven its methods aren't working. For centuries girls have fought one another and grown into women who fight each other. If we want the madness to stop, we have to try something new by trying something old. Try the proverb and see if it doesn't prove true.

So what does this mean to you, popular girl? Well, what's the most important thing to most girls in high school? Their reputation. Bad reputation, bad life. Good reputation, good life, for the most part. So help her build her rep. Give her the gift of good gossip. Since you are the popular girl, you have the most power and maybe even the most responsibility to control social change in your school. What you say, people listen to. So here's what you can do. Tell people good stuff about the Mean Girl. Now don't make it up, because you'll look like an idiot, but tell them things that are true. If you like her unique style, then tell people. If you think she has great hair, then tell people. Talk her up, make her look good to others, and help her to be elevated in the friend chain. She'll soon get wind of it and might not have a clue why you are doing it, and that will either shock her into kindness or freak her out so much she'll just leave you alone. In fact, if you are really brave, you could even try complimenting her when you know she can hear you. Nothing is better than overhearing someone talking nicely about you. It's addictive; you just want to hear more. So test the truth and see if it doesn't work.

If you keep doing what you've done, you'll keep getting what you've got. Is that good enough?

Now don't expect her to instantly want to be best friends with you. She might hate you for the rest of her life, but you can't control that. All you can control is your own mouth, your own life, and your own destiny. Be the best you can be without worrying if it changes other people, and you will win in the end. Even if her torture never stops, you win. So decide today who you want to be and then be that girl, not the girl she is trying to make you be.

Give her the gift of good gossip.

If you have a really nice body and all the guys really like you, look out for Mean Girls. You'll be on the top of their list (as if you didn't already know that). Again, it's because you are an easy target. In fact, your existence almost begs them to harass you, because if they can make you look bad, then they come up a rung on the beauty ladder. It's just like your mother said: *"They're just jealous."* It's true, but that doesn't help you, does it?

Okay, so they make the choice to hate you. But what is the solution? What can you do when you're too hot for the other girls? And before you say, *"I'm not hot,"* let me just say that hot girls never *think* they're hot. But it's always what others think. And if you do think you're oh-so-hot, then you might want to tone down your self-appreciation just a bit. That might be what's making them all hate you. But if you are just hated because of your looks and you aren't parading around like a princess, then what can you do? How can you cope?

1. **Compliment them.** First, know that you can't change them, only love them. (Note: Love might make them kinder, but it's not your job to change them, only to love them. See *God's Plan for Your Mean Girl,* page 115.) If they feel insecure and ugly, you can't change that. No matter what you do. People's feelings are controlled by them, not you. So don't kid yourself into thinking you can control a change in them. You can try to help raise their self-image, but you have no power over whether they accept it or not. But **just like the popular girl,** you the hot girl **pull some weight on campus.** You have power that you might not really be aware of. So saying something nice about the Mean Girl is a big win for both of you. If you haven't read it yet, go back and read *The Popular Girl* (page 59). Seriously, it will give you great ideas about reaching out to the Mean Girl. So

stop now, go back and read, and I'll be here when you get back. It's way important!

2. **Control yourself.** You have the power to control yourself. You can decide what you are going to do about their reactions to you. If you've decided that you want to be the girl you were made to be, then you know you can't choose revenge. You can't take their anger and return it, because it's not gonna help you be the pure, good, faithful girl you were made to be. (Check out *The Mean Girl Cycle*, page 80.)

3. **Let it slide.** Your only other choice is to let it slide. Think of yourself like a duck and their comments like water. You can swim right through them and they will never get through to your skin; they just slide off because you know they aren't true. You know the truth, and what they are sayin' ain't it. This takes a lot of hard work and concentration, and some days you will think you just can't handle it any longer, but let me give you some hope:

"God blesses the people who patiently endure testing. Afterward they will receive the crown of life that God has promised to those who love him" (James chapter 1, verse 12 NLT).

"Dear friends, don't be surprised at the fiery trials you are going through, as if something strange were happening to you" (1 Peter chapter 4, verse 12 NLT).

"If you think you are standing strong, be careful, for you, too, may fall into the same sin. But remember that the temptations that come into your life are no different from what others experience. And

God is faithful. He will keep the temptation from becoming so strong that you can't stand up against it. When you are tempted, he will show you a way out so that you will not give in to it" (1 Corinthians chapter 10, verses 12–13 NLT).

"So you see, the Lord knows how to rescue godly people from their trials, even while punishing the wicked right up until the day of judgment. He is especially hard on those who follow their own evil, lustful desires and who despise authority. These people are proud and arrogant, daring even to scoff at the glorious ones without so much as trembling" (2 Peter chapter 2, verses 9–10 NLT).

Also check out *Why Are You So Easy to Hate?* on page 75.

THE SHY GIRL

The shy girl is in an odd position because the way she acts looks a lot like the stuck-up hot girl. Think about it. The similarities are striking, not necessarily in outward appearances but in behavior. The stuck-up hot girl walks right by you and doesn't say a word, as if she's just too good for you. Shy girl, you do the same. You walk right by and don't say a word to anyone. The stuck-up hot girl doesn't sit by people in class and just start talking to them, 'cause she's too good for that, but neither does the shy girl. You just sit down and keep your eyes on your desk. Yeah, the stuck-up girl and the shy girl look a lot alike to the outside viewer. And that might be why they pick on you—not because you're shy but because they think you are just plain stuck-up. Mean Girls don't really take time to think; they just react. So when you don't smile at them, you avoid eye contact, and you never interact with them, they say to themselves, "Gee, she isn't very nice. Won't even smile at me. She must think she's too good for me." And their temperature rises. How could *you* think you are too good for *her*? You clearly aren't any better, she thinks, and bam!, she's off to prove it. It's simply a case of you being another easy target. You become, in her mind, a Mean Girl who needs to be taught a lesson. You need to learn to notice her like the rest of the world.

Now you, on the other hand, are just unbearably shy. You don't feel anywhere near as important or as good as the other girls, so you hide. You hide in a crowd, you hide all alone, you hide any way you can. You hide your eyes from theirs and your heart as well. I know, it's a big, dangerous world out there. And believe me, I know what it's like to be shy. In middle school and the first part of high school, I was the shy girl. I didn't know anyone in school because I had just moved to town in 7th grade. I didn't think anyone could possibly like me or want to talk to me, so I kept to myself. By 9th grade the girls assumed that I thought I was just too good for them, but that wasn't true at all. **I was scared of them.** I was insecure and not able to express myself. I came from a family of women who never interacted with other women. Having friends wasn't something we ever did. So I had no idea how to be a friend. And I was ostracized and made fun of by more social girls.

Now that I'm older and can look back with less pain on my growing up years, I realize that I could have done a few things differently that would have changed my life back then. One of them is that **I could have known Christ**, and that would have made all the difference in the world. See, knowing him would have meant that I could have confidence. Confidence that I was called to love others no matter how ill-equipped I felt. Confidence that life wasn't about me; it was about serving him and those he put in my life. The other thing I could have done is that **I could have gotten over myself** and made more of an effort to make friends. I could have trusted Jesus enough to help me to find and nurture friendships. Oh, if I only knew then what I know now!

If you have a Mean Girl, I pray that you know Christ, because he is really your salvation, in more ways than one. It's simple, really: This amazing God sent his one and only Son to die for you so that all your sins, all your junk, would be forever erased. He sent him so that you could have direct access to the God of the universe, and because of him you do. And with that salvation that he gave you by dying on a cross and covering up all your junk with his blood, you have a new set of rules to live by. You aren't the same girl you used to be. You have a bigger purpose. You have a mission. You were created for something, and now you know it. The world isn't about cliques and fighting. It isn't about who's the most popular or the smartest. It's about him. How can you serve him as a soldier in his army? How do you come into the fullness of who you are, not who they are?

When you accept your position as a child of the King through the death and resurrection of Christ, an amazing thing happens—your agenda dies with him. It's called dying to self, and it's an amazing freedom. It's a set of wings that will allow you to soar high above their pettiness and see your role in saving and serving these girls. You aren't alive to be hurt and fearful; you are alive to be a power in the world. You are alive to be used mightily by a living God. If you realize your position, that he lives in you, and that he desperately loves these girls, then you begin to have the power to break out of yourself, to break out of being shy, and to love them the way he called you to. Remember, this life isn't about you and your fears; it's about your God and his plans for you. It's about loving him and loving them just because he loved you. So here's what I want you to do: I want you to power up. I want you to first realize who you are and then start to act like it.

> This life isn't about you and your fears; it's about your God and his plans for you.

1. **Pray this with me:** Father, I am alone and lonely in this world. I have nothing in and of myself and I know it. I have repeatedly failed in your sight and mine. But I'm thankful that you sent your Son to die a terrible death on a dirty cross just because you loved me so much. I accept that death and believe in the resurrection. I want to turn away from my bad ways and love you completely as Lord of my life. Thank you for designing me to be used in a big way by you. Thank you for loving me unconditionally. Today I accept that love and will walk in it. Thank you, Father. Amen.

2. **To-do list.** Now that we've gotten that taken care of, here is your assignment. I want you to learn about who your God is and who you are. No more lies, no more fears. You have a job to do, so it's time to get over yourself and start to love not only your friends but also your enemies. So get yourself a Bible and look up these verses. Write them down, learn them, and keep them with you always: Romans 10:9; Romans 3:22–24; Romans 8:15, 31–33; Romans 12:9–21; Galatians 5:24; Ephesians 6:12; Mark 12:29–31. (If you need more, turn to the end of this book and start looking up the verses there. There's plenty for all you need.)

3. **Learn to love.** If you haven't read it, then go back to *The Outsider* on page 55 and read #4, *Learn to Love*. This stuff applies to you too. So go, go read it. You'll love it, I promise.

For more help, check out *God's Plan for Your Mean Girl* on page 115 and *Why Are You So Easy to Hate?* on page 75.

*The book of Proverbs, chapter 27, verse 4: "Anger is cruel and fury overwhelming, but who can stand before jealousy?"

What a burden intelligence is! You can't help it, you're just smart, so how can they hold it against you? But they do. It all comes down to jealousy. It's an evil thing.* But it's a normal thing in a fallen world. People who don't know Christ as a best friend, who don't know Christ as their comforter and their protection, have only themselves to save them, and that's a scary thought. So when they see someone who has more than they have, they panic. They have to protect themselves, so they fight back. And if your Mean Girl is a "Christian," then it's really too bad, because she should know better. Jealousy does not make God happy. It's against his law (Romans 13:13). And she should have enough hope in him not to need to attack you to make herself feel better. But alas, she doesn't, so now the question is, What do you do? You are smart; you can't change that, and who would want to? Smart is good.

But I wish there were a verse that said, "Be smart and do not sin." See, sometimes we can be so smart that we sin. And what I mean by that is that we are so smart that we allow our smartness to make us judgmental of others who aren't as smart as us. We don't have patience for people who just don't get it. Believe me, I understand this. I happen to be someone who gets stuff really quickly. I am a quick learner, and I admit that I've gotten very steamed at people who are slower than me. I mean, I got it, why can't they? I huff and I puff, wishing they would hurry up and get it. I've hurt many of my friends and family members by being frustrated with their inability to get things that I already got, and that's just plain ugly. I have confessed this to them, and I am making every effort to avoid frustration with "stupid" people, but it's hard. See, I just called them "stupid," and they aren't! They are just different. And deep down I know that, but I make them feel stupid because I think I'm so smart.

Now I'm not saying you're a little cocky. I'm not even saying you're Little Miss Smarty-Pants. But remember, your brains were a gift; you didn't make yourself smart. That doesn't mean that others won't resent you for it, though. So what can you do (besides shutting off your brain)? In some cases you might be doing everything right. You might not be huffy when others don't get it. You might not be a teacher's pet, or Little Miss Know-It-All. (But if you are, then let me just say, Bingo! We found out why they hate you. Get over yourself!) They have no right to hate you, but hate you they do, so how will you cope?

The nature of humans is envy and covetousness. That's why God's law speaks against it. The reason it even has to be written about is that it's natural. What's not natural is the opposite—being happy for other people's gifts and caring about their happiness. Girl, you are in a unique position by being smart. That means that you can be used in ways that many others will never be used. You have the ability to comprehend things and achieve things that will rock this world.

But if you spend all your time worrying about what other girls think of you, you will never get there. God has a plan for you, a purpose. He gave you a passion that burns deep in your soul. I want to tell you 2 things about that passion. The 1st is that it's an amazing thing, and you should not let hate or meanness get in the way of doing what you were called to do. And 2nd, you should also not let your passion, your dream, get in the way of what you are called to do—and that is to love your enemies. Use your brain to figure out ways to help others. Don't make yourself dumber to help them. Help them at the same time that you help yourself. See, you have 2 missions: to live your passion and to love others. You can't give up on either. So use that big brain of yours and figure out how to love people who don't love you back. Start with this list.

1. **Look at what God has to say** about your enemy. Check out Proverbs 24:17–18; Romans 12:14; Zechariah 7:10; Matthew 5:44; Exodus 23:4; Luke 6:27; Romans 12:20.

2. **Don't try to be the teacher's pet.** You alienate yourself from the rest of the class when you side with the teacher. Try to love everyone equally and don't get all manipulative with the teacher by making her like you most. That's just playing dirty.

3. **Help.** Help other people study. If you are smart, then give your time to help people who don't get it.

4. **Take it with a grain of salt.** You are smart, and for the rest of your life you will face girls who hate you because of it. Don't act dumb to please them. Don't be mean. Just be who you are. In the end you will be honored and loved deeply by your God, and that is what really counts.

THE CONFIDENT GIRL

I always teach girls that confidence is the sexiest thing about a girl, and evidence of that is when Mean Girls hate you. If confidence wasn't so appealing, the Mean Girl wouldn't be jealous, but it is and she is. Confidence comes from a steady trust that God has you where you should be, when you should be there, and that he's got everything under control (go back to Romans 8:28!). It shows in your demeanor because you are at peace, and people are often jealous of that because most of them aren't at peace. Confidence isn't a bad thing; it's simply the recognition that you are who God made you to be and that is enough—no, that's more than enough. It's a beautiful thing, so others envy you for having something they don't.

So what can you do? Act insecure to please them? Cut yourself down? Complain about your big nose or wide behind? No, that would be dishonoring to the God who made your big nose and wide behind (1 Corinthians chapter 6, verses 19 and 20). Never give up your confidence for anyone, even if it will gain you access to the inner circle. It isn't worth it. But there are some things you can do. If you are confident, know that there will always be girls who hate you because you have what they desperately want. That never goes away. Jealousy sucks. But there are some things you can try to help ease the pain.

1. **Love 'em.** If you are so confident, then it shouldn't be hard for you to do this one thing: Love your enemy. Ugh! I know, how horrific, but how holy. Read all about it in Proverbs 24:17–18; Romans 12:14; Zechariah 7:10; Matthew 5:44; Exodus 23:4; Luke 6:27; Romans 12:20. Use your confidence to help others. Invite the Mean Girl over for a swim. Get to know her one-on-one. Help her with her homework. Do what you can to honor your God. She might not ever respond to your kindness, but this isn't about the outcome. It's about you serving your God the way he's called you to serve. Don't expect big changes in her, just in you. You are the only one you can control. But risk this for your God—risk loving someone who hates you. Love isn't about how you "feel." God never commanded you to feel good about your Mean Girls (enemies), only to love them. Love isn't a feeling; it is a choice. If it were a feeling, God couldn't have commanded you to do it, because feelings can't be ordered around.

2. **React to her attacks with love,** or at least humor. You are confident, so you can keep your cool when she attacks. If she says something mean to you, don't get mad. Just smile and say something funny, or nothing at all. Remember, you lose when she makes you mad. So no matter what, don't get mad.

As you see, girls find all kinds of reasons to hate other girls. But regardless of why your particular Mean Girl decided she didn't like you, your reaction to her is clear. If you love God and you want to be obedient to him, then you have only one option, and that is love. Love can mean all kinds of things, but it is always selfless. Whatever form your love takes, remember

Check out *Degrees of Mean* (page 21) and *What Do You Do If You Are Popular and a Target of Mean Girls?* (page 59) to find out more ways to keep your cool.

> "Therefore, he who rejects this instruction does not reject man but God, who gives you his Holy Spirit."
>
> 1 Thessalonians chapter 4, verse 8

that it isn't about you and your image but about God and his hand in your life. **Will you let the Mean Girl win** and make you disobedient to God's call to love your enemy, or will you rise above her goading and prove yourself faithful?

Why Are You So Easy to Hate?

The story goes that in a land far away lived an old man. Every day he sat at the city gate and talked to passersby. One day a young man came by with a pack on his back. The old man smiled at the young man, who sat down beside him. He looked tired and dirty. "I'm looking for a new city," he said to the old man. "What is this one like? Are the people nice here?" he asked. The old man looked at the young man for a few moments and then said, "What were the people like in the city you have come from?" The young man looked down and sighed, "Oh, they were horrible, cruel people. Always out to get me and ruin my life. That is why I left. I couldn't stand them any longer."

"Well, that is exactly the kind of people you shall find here," the old man said. "You'd best be on your way, because you won't be happy here either." And with that the young man got up and left for the next city.

A few hours later a young girl walked up to the old man and said, "Excuse me, sir, I am looking for a new town to call my home, and I was wondering if you can tell me anything about the people who live here." The old man looked at the girl and smiled. Then he said, "What were the people like in the city you have come from?" The young girl smiled and said, "Oh, they were very kind. They always looked after me and cared for me. I liked them very much." The old man looked down and smiled as he said, "You shall find the same sort of people here, my dear. Kind and caring. Enter the city and find yourself home."

You get what you are looking for.

The old man didn't need to tell either of the passersby what *he* thought of the people of the town. He just asked them what they expected based on their last town. See, you get what you are looking for. Expect people to be mean to you, and they will most certainly be mean. I know it seems like some kind of New

Age mumbo jumbo that you get what you expect to get—it's not that, but it is true. Our forefathers knew that long before we did. In the ancient text of Proverbs, the author says that what a man thinks, he gets (read Proverbs 23:7 in the KJV). The way you see the world is the way the world will be for you.

> "When anyone provokes you, remember that it is your own opinion about him that provokes you. Try not to be tossed around by appearances."
> —Epectitus

Okay, so cut back to you, the loner girl at school. You're alone, defensive, angry at the world. They've hurt you, and you aren't going to let them forget it. I know the pain is unbearable and sometimes you don't want to go on, but there is a way around it, a way through it. Follow me close here: People will treat you the way you expect to be treated. So if Bobby Jo walks up and says, "Nice dress," you have two responses:

1. You look at her, snarl, and say angrily, "Whatever!" I mean, you know she has it out for you, and you won't take it, so slam her back. Don't take any of her crap.

2. You choose to look her in the eyes, smile, and say, "Gee, thanks. I like yours too." I mean, you don't know what she meant by that comment, so why not assume she meant what she said? And who knows, if you're nice, she might actually leave you alone. She gets no points from the nice girl, just from the angry one.

Okay, so let's recap. You get angry, you lose. She makes you mad, she gets a point. You smile and don't get upset, *you* get the point. And on the game goes. Now, eventually, if you keep up the second option, you will have so many points that it will be a landslide victory and she will get out while the losing is good. No points, no reason to stick around and play. She isn't necessarily going to lay off right away, but like I said, the more points you can get by *not* getting mad, the less interesting as prey you become.

> The **goal** of the Mean Girl is to **make you mad**. Every time you get mad, she gets a point.

And pretty soon she'll be off to find easier pickings. It's the law of the jungle. Or maybe you'll even be able to rid the world of one more Mean Girl.

you
and your
Mean
Girl

The Mean Girl Cycle: "She Started It!"

You're not a Mean Girl. You don't go around looking for a fight. You aren't bad. You're just a normal girl. If someone slams you or steals your boyfriend, then sure, you want to get even. And who says there is anything wrong with that? I mean, she started it. A girl has to protect herself. You can't just stand by while people walk all over you, right? Don't you have a right to get even when another girl totally starts it and is just asking for you to do something about it? Have a gander at this list and tell me your honest opinion. Which of these four situations do you relate to?

3-Way Call/IM—Your so-called "friend" is spreading rumors about you. You guys are totally close, so you are completely shocked when you find out she's telling people that you are a loser. She is really nice to your face. You guys eat lunch together. You go to her house after school a lot. You're buds, so why is she doing this? It's best to just find out, isn't it? So you take matters into your own hands to find out what the heck is going on. Friday night while you are at her house, you ask her, "Do you think I'm a loser?" She tells you, "Of course not! I think you're very cool. Why would you say that?" And you drop it because she's obviously not coming clean. But still you wonder. So on Monday, you call up another friend and ask her if she will **do a 3-way call** for you so you can find out what's really going on. That night your 2nd friend calls your 1st friend while you listen in. She starts talking about you and probing the other girl to find out what she *really* thinks about you.

Slam Doc—A girl in your class has a smart mouth. She just loves to slam you whenever she gets the chance. She's funny, so everyone laughs at her. And by the way, they laugh at you too. How humiliating. So you decide to get even. You need a smear campaign that will totally prove to her that you are liked way more than her. So you start a petition going around. You get all your friends to sign a sheet that says all kinds of bad stuff about her. They all agree that she's a mean old hag and sign your petition. Pretty soon you have pages full of hate signatures agreeing that this chick is evil.

Smear Campaign—The hot girl on campus totally took your boyfriend from you, and now it's get even time. It's not that you hate her, it's just that what she did was wrong, so you're gonna let everyone know about. You start to tell all your friends what a cow she is and what a horrible thing she did. Then you go to the next table and tell all of them. You've started your own smear campaign. Just wait, she'll be sorry that she messed with your man!

Blogging—The new girl in school took your spot on the volleyball team, and now she's moving in on your boyfriend. You want to find a way to show him that she's a total witch, so you write a story about the time she lied about you and made you look bad in front of the coach. You blog your little story about how horrible she really is for all to see.

The list could go on and on. Another girl does something to you, so you retaliate. It only seems fair. I mean, what are you supposed to do, just sit there and take it? If a girl starts it, then you're gonna finish it. But what tools do you use in your retaliation? When another girl starts something, what becomes fair game? Check all the things from this list that you'd like to use to get her back.

☐ tell people what she did
☐ 3-way call on her

- ☐ create a slam doc
- ☐ tell on her to an adult
- ☐ get her in trouble
- ☐ start a rumor
- ☐ tell everyone how mean she is
- ☐ make fun of her
- ☐ TP her house
- ☐ egg her car
- ☐ hate her
- ☐ tell your friends not to like her
- ☐ other: _____

If you checked any of these and think that if she starts it, you can finish it, let me ask you a simple question: Has anyone done any of those things to you? Did it hurt? Don't just skim over this question. Think about it.

Did it hurt when someone did these things to you?

Was it mean when they did it?

If you would say, "Yes, it was mean when they did that to me," but you think it's still okay for *you* to do it, does that make *you* mean? Are you mean if you do mean things like these? Or are you just being you, and it's only mean when *they* do it? Think about that answer very carefully, dear one. You have to be honest with yourself if you want to face your own beast. If you've thought about it and you see my point—mean is as mean does—then be honest with God and check this box.

☐ **I am a Mean Girl.**

Check this box if you confess that you have been a Mean Girl at any time in the past.

So are you? Are you a Mean Girl? Have you been one at any time in the past? Did you check the box? If you did, congratulations on admitting it, because I think we're all mean at one time or another. And if you thought that anything from that list of retaliations was okay, then you're a Mean Girl. I know, that sounds harsh. I mean, how can you be mean? You're *you!* You're nice. And besides, you never started it. *She's* the mean one, not you.

Think about it like this. Say I start playing volleyball by hitting the ball to you over the net, and you hit it back, and we keep hitting it back and forth. There is no way you can say to me, "But I'm not playing volleyball, 'cuz you started it." How ridiculous. Of course you are playing! It doesn't matter who served; you are still playing. It doesn't matter who started it; you're still mean. See, my precious one, if you join in on her meanness, then you too are mean. I know you don't want to be. I know you are nice, and I know that you are hurt by the stuff she does. But when you hit back, you are playing the game. You are joining in on the mean, and by default you become a Mean Girl.

> Most of us have been mean. The question is, will we continue to be mean?

Now, I believe in you. I don't think that you want to be mean. You just didn't realize that you *were* mean. It's part of girl world to fight with each other. It's a dog-eat-dog world out there, and you have to protect yourself. Believe me, I understand. But since I know that you don't want to be mean and that you do want to be holy, let me help you out on this. To be mean, even as revenge, is still to be mean. And not only is that bad, but the revenge part itself is dangerous territory. It's stealing. Yep, you read it right, revenge is stealing—and it's not just ordinary stealing, it's stealing from God. Eek! Not a good thing. Not a guy to mess with.

See, in his Word God says "Vengeance is mine." Oops, did you miss that? Check it out, in the book of Deuteronomy, chapter 32, verse 35 in the New King James Version of the Bible, God says, *"Vengeance is mine."* And in *The Message,* a paraphrase of the Bible by Eugene Peterson, the verse says, *"I'm in charge of vengeance and payback."* Did you catch that? It's God's job, not yours, to get even with people. The second that you go for revenge, you steal from God by taking the vengeance that is his. And think about this: *Revenge is defined as an opportunity for getting satisfaction, for getting even.* The moment you seek revenge, you are self-seeking. You are looking out for yourself and trying to get satisfaction. That flies in the face of all that is holy, righteous, and good. Perhaps you don't know this, but as a child of God you are called to:

sacrifice yourself (Romans 12:1)
think of others rather than yourself (Romans 12:10)
take care of your enemies (Proverbs 25:21)
love your enemies (Matthew 5:44)
not repay evil with evil (1 Peter 3:8–9; Proverbs 20:22)
trust God to judge (1 Peter 2:23)
forgive (Proverbs 17:9)

If you still think you have a right to revenge, then please explain. In the space on the next page, write down how revenge fulfills any of the callings I listed above.

vengeance = punishment inflicted in retaliation for an injury or offense

revenge = an opportunity for getting satisfaction

My revenge is holy because _____
_____.

If you want to stop the cycle of mean, then start today. Write down why revenge is evil and then make a commitment never again to seek what isn't yours.

Revenge is evil because _____
_____.

My commitment: _____
_____.

If you want to let God have back his vengeance, you think he can do it better than you anyway, and you want to be a holy girl, then read this prayer out loud right now.

Father, today I commit to being holy. I choose to follow your Word rather than my emotions. I will not be self-seeking. I will love those who hate me. And I will trust you to take care of the situation. I will overlook offenses, and I will practice love rather than retaliation. I want to stop the cycle of mean. I want you to be proud of me. I want to be proud of me. Thank you for forgiving me for all the mean stuff I have done in my life. Today I make a clean break. Today I will learn to love the world the way you do.

If you prayed this out loud, I am proud of you. I know it's hard to say that you've been mean, so I'm proud of you for admitting it. That's the first step in stopping the cycle of mean. From now on ask yourself, *Is what I am wanting to do love or hate? Is this from the Father or from the enemy?* If you choose love, God will help you through the trials that the other girl has brought you into. Trust him and he will make you holy.

Revenge is defined as an opportunity for getting satisfaction, for getting even. The moment you seek revenge, you are self-seeking.

Getting Even Is Getting Mean

Okay, now it's time to think. Time to ponder and get real. Check yourself:

1. How many times while you were reading this book have you had a memory pop into your head of a time when you faced a Mean Girl? _____
2. How many times while reading this book have you had a flashback of *you* getting revenge on a Mean Girl? _____
3. How many times have you 3-way called to get some info on someone? _____
4. Have you ever gossiped about a girl you didn't like? Yes   No
5. Do you know girls who really deserve to be put in their place?   Yes   No
6. Think about the girls in your life. Would any of them say that you had been mean to them?   Yes   No

When I go to schools I talk about "the mean effect." I go up to the board and draw a simple little diagram that shows how mean moves from girl to girl. See, mean is a living, breathing thing that grows the more it's fed. It lives off the attention of girls just like you. When a girl is mean to you, you feel hurt, mad, angry, and bitter, and you convince yourself that she needs to hurt as bad as you—that somehow if she does, you'll feel a ton better. So you get to work getting even, and the cycle begins. Pretty soon the world is spinning in mean, and all because you took step 2 and retaliated.

Diagram A: She's mean to you.

You   Mean Girl

Diagram B: *You're mean to her.*

You   Mean Girl

Diagram C: *She's mean back, and the cycle continues.*

You   Mean Girl

See the cycle? So now that it's going like this, how can you stop her from being mean? Think about it. Okay, I'll give you the answer. What if you stopped your arrow to her? That would stop at least the momentum of the cycle. The trouble with Mean Girls is that some of them aren't mean for fun but are mean for a reason. They are mean because they feel like *you* deserve it, just like you are mean back because you feel *they* deserve it. These diagrams show how you really become *her* Mean Girl. See, it doesn't matter *why* you are mean. If she took your boyfriend, or told on you, or gossiped about you, and you decide you now have a *reason* to be mean, you are still mean. Even if it's because "she started it." In fact, the next time you utter the words, "but she started it," I want you to remember that those 4 words just made you a Mean Girl. Welcome to the wonderful world of mean—how do you like it? Are you proud of yourself? Is God smiling? Harsh questions, I know—sometimes I just get a little sassy. But you catch my drift. Getting even is getting mean.

Let me put it like this: When you get even, you give the other girl power over you. You just let her crawl into your heart and carve a piece out of it. You have taken the first step in shaping your heart into one just like hers. Getting

"But she started it!" = "I'm a Mean Girl!"

even means getting her in your system. You know how it feels. She becomes your obsession. You think about her all day. You plot. You talk. You plan. She's in your system, and in fact, the thought of her is running your system. Ick! The very girl you detest is now in charge of your system.

I can hear you screaming inside, "No, she's not! I'm in charge, and I'm getting her back!" Okay, keep on lying to yourself like we girls just love to do. I guess it's like Jack Nicholson said in *A Few Good Men*: "You can't handle the truth!" The truth is, when you get even, you lose, but that makes you mad. Somehow it doesn't seem fair. She can hurt you, but you can't hurt her back? Yup. If you think that getting even is an excuse to be mean, you are lying, and believing a lie is stupid, especially if it's one told by yourself.

Next Steps

repent: to feel regret, to change your mind

If you look at what we just did and say, "Dang, I don't like that fact about me. I want to be free from meanness," and you really, really mean it, then there's only one thing left to do: repent.

Repenting just means that you tell God, "I hate being like that, and I don't want to do it anymore." Then you walk away from it. You determine that from now on when meany is mean to you, you won't retaliate. You won't continue the cycle. You will decide today who you want to be and follow through on that. It's a lot easier to stick to your guns when you decide what to do in advance. Make a game plan. Figure out how you will be nice. Carry verses with you to read when your blood pressure rises and you want to destroy her. Refuse to think evil thoughts even when she really deserves them. Make a list of what you will and won't do. Make it today so that tomorrow you will know how to respond. That's repentance—deciding to stop whatever it was you were doing that wasn't right. So give it a shot. Here's your chance.

The next time my Mean Girl says something mean to my face, I will _____.

If a Mean Girl takes my boyfriend or even just makes a pass at him, I will _____.

I promise that I will not (circle the ones you won't do any longer):

get revenge   lie about her   try to control her

gossip   slam her

3-way call   hate

I agree with the following prayer: Yes   No

Father, I don't want to be a Mean Girl. I want to be a godly girl who loves my enemies. I promise to forgive, no matter what. I promise to trust you with justice, and I won't try to get revenge myself. I will no longer talk about other girls in a mean way but will build them up. I promise not to 3-way call to find out secret information. I will not write slam letters or tell others how much I hate a person. And I will trust you to manage the lives of my friends. I won't try to control them or manipulate them to my advantage. Today I promise to be a godly girl and to always love and never hate. Amen.*

If you are really ready to repent and turn away from mean, you might want to pray these prayers for your Mean Girl.

*The godly girl refuses to resort to meanness ever again as a show of devotion and love to the Father.

◼ Prayer of Forgiveness

Papa God, I confess that I have not been a godly girl. I have done things that are mean and have hurt other girls. I confess that I am not living the way you call me to live. I have not loved the way I am supposed to love. I have sinned and done what is evil in your sight, and I am truly sorry to have done that to you. I no longer want to be mean in any way, because you are not pleased when I am mean. Today I commit my heart to you and trust you to help me be nice. Thank you for the forgiveness you promise to give when we confess. I am thankful that you are so kind and loving to me. Thank you, Father. Amen.

◼ Prayer for the Mean Girl

Dear Father, I want to pray for _____. I know that she must be hurting, and I know you don't want any of your creation to hurt. Father, I confess that I haven't loved her, but I want to love her, so I pray for her. I pray that she would come to know you intimately and that her love for you would overflow onto others. I pray that you would soothe her aches and pains and fill her with your Holy Spirit. Please draw her closer to you where she can find safety. Give her peace and hope and love. I pray that she would come to know you so well that she would make a big difference in the world for you. Help her to see me in your light and to learn to love rather than hate. I pray also that I would learn how to love her the way you do. Thank you for hearing this prayer. I love you, Father. Amen.

Why Does It Feel Good to Be Mean?

Being mean feels good sometimes. You know it does. But why does it feel so good just to slam someone? Or to put them in their place? Or to get even and make them squirm? What is in us that makes us feel good to be mean? I can't speak for you, but I can speak for myself and the times when I've been a Mean Girl. I remember feeling like I wanted to teach them a lesson. **Punishing them almost felt like a noble cause.** A pastor once told me, "Hayley, you like to play God, and he isn't pleased." Ouch. Me, I like to play God? Well, maybe he was right. I guess I used to think that God needed help. That he couldn't punish those Mean Girls enough, so I should be his instrument and do some of it for him. I mean, after all, I knew how bad they hurt me, so I was the best girl for the job of convicting and sentencing them.

Trouble is, even in the world, when someone is charged with a crime, the victim doesn't get to sit as judge and jury on the trial. No, she just gets to plead her side of the case and then pray that the judge and jury make good decisions as to the punishment for the crime. So why do we think it's our job to judge the Mean Girls in our lives and dole out the punishment for them like Judge Judy having an afternoon of fun? I have found that if I don't assume I know people's motives and I don't jump to conclusions on punishment for them, my life works out much better. Half the time I find out they didn't mean it the way I took it, and the other half I just lose interest and the cycle stops. So over the years I've learned that the best thing to do is to **deny the good feeling of being mean** and instead to soak up the awful feeling of being broken. Brokenness is that feeling you get when you tell your pride to shut up and trust God. It's that awful pain in your gut you get when you tell yourself, "It doesn't matter what they think," even though deep down you feel like it does. The whole process of dying to your sinful self is a painful one, but just like lifting weights, there is no gain if there is no pain. I believe that the girl who cannot die to self can never accomplish what her heart desires.

So the next time that being mean sounds really good to you, check yourself. Do you want to go down that path, or do you want to grow stronger and stronger in your spirit? Will you give up who you want to be just to experience mean? Or will you die to self so that you might grow in faith, hope, and love?

I believe that the girl who cannot die to self can never accomplish what her heart desires.

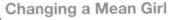

Changing a Mean Girl

We've worked on you, so now it's time to think about Little Miss Meany. You can try lots of ways to win over a Mean Girl (see the advice in *Why Does She Hate You?* starting on page 55). But one thing you have to consider is that you might never, ever win her over. That doesn't mean you failed; it just means that she's not ready. Changing her isn't your job, but loving your enemies and forgiving people is. When a soul loves and forgives, it soars to freedom on wings like eagles. But a soul bound to revenge and bitterness sinks to the depths of the sea and lives forever bound by the ties of self.

> What doesn't destroy me makes me stronger.

So when it comes to your Mean Girl, focus on what you are to do instead of what you think she should do or become. Don't look for an outcome; just keep your eye on the process of you becoming the woman you were made to be. How will you ever prove who you are? How will you ever prove your strength if you don't go through tough battles in life? Each attack that you live through and, more than that, *love* through, is a victory for your soul. Think of your soul like a big round diamond in the rough, and imagine that each blow that she throws at you and you absorb rather than retaliate is hitting the rough and knocking off another bit. As you grow, your diamond will become more and more brilliant as the dull pieces are chipped away to reveal the shimmering pure center.

You are a girl with power. You are a free spirit who has the willpower and ability to choose your destiny. A road paved with bitterness and resentment will lead you to a life of depression and agony. But if you pave your road with hope and love, your spirit will soar, and you will rise above the rest as a daughter of the King. Your strength of spirit will be obvious to everyone. They will applaud you, they will want to be around you, and they will want to be like you. Only those who have suffered great loss truly are prepared to lead the rest of us to victory. Only those who have felt the flaming arrows of anger and jealousy and chosen not to return them are fully prepared to serve a living King.

Your goal in life should not be to change evil people and not to stop their attacks but to follow the King. If you keep your eye on the prize instead of on the enemy, you will change more hearts and impact more people than you ever could with your own strength. If your most important goal is to love the King and to know him more, then take this attack from the enemy as a call for a step *toward* God, not *away from* him. Remember, the enemy loses. Read the book called Revelation, 'cause it is a real revelation—he loses. It's right there in the 20th chapter and the 10th verse: LOSER. So your tormentors are inconsequential in the grand scheme of things. Their only real purpose is to drive you either closer to or farther from God. Which will it be? Will you whine, worry, fret, fear, and seek revenge, or will you rise above, dismiss the enemy and his powerlessness, and surround yourself with praises for your King? The choice is yours, my sister. Choose wisely.

[For my determined purpose is] that I may know Him [that I may progressively become more deeply and intimately acquainted with Him, perceiving and recognizing and understanding the wonders of His Person more strongly and more clearly], and that I may in that same way come to know the power outflowing from His resurrection [which it exerts over believers], and that I may so share His sufferings as to be continually transformed [in spirit into His likeness even] to His death.

Paul's letter to the Philippians, chapter 3, verse 10 AMP

"You're **blessed** when you're at the end of your rope. With less of you there is more of God and his rule. You're blessed when you feel you've lost what is most dear to you. Only then can you be embraced by the One most dear to you. You're blessed when you're content with just who you are—no more, no less. That's the moment you find yourselves proud owners of everything that can't be bought. . . . You're blessed when **you care**. At the moment of being 'carefull,' you find yourselves cared for. . . . You're blessed when you can show people how to cooperate instead of compete or fight. That's when you discover who you really are, and your place in God's family. You're blessed when your commitment to God provokes persecution. The persecution drives you even deeper into God's kingdom. Not only that—count yourselves **blessed every time people put you down** or throw you out or speak lies about you to discredit me. What it means is that the truth is too close for comfort and they are uncomfortable. You can be glad when that happens—give a cheer, even!—for though they don't like it, I do! And all heaven applauds."

Matthew chapter 5, verses 3–5, 7,
and 9–12, MESSAGE

So Offended

When it comes to the things that mean people do, a lot of times I hear girls say, "I was just so offended by what she said." Girls, this might come as a shock, but I am here to tell you that as a believer, being offended is not okay.

What? That's right. If you are offended by anything girls are saying about you, then you are caring more about yourself than about God. Let me explain.

If you are a believer, your goal is the same as mine: You want to be more like Christ, right? I know that sometimes that seems impossibly hard; in fact, most of the time it *is* impossibly hard. But it's what you want to do. It's who you are. And what's more, it's what *he* wants you to do and who he made you to be. And in deciding to become more like Christ, one big thing that a lot of people miss about imitating him is that he was not offended for himself. Jesus even said, "Father, forgive them, for they do not know what they are doing" (Luke chapter 23, verse 34).

In fact, only one thing offended him to the point of action, and that was *when people offended his Father*. Jesus had a lot of mean things done to him. People accused him of stuff he didn't do, beat him, put nails in his hands, and then told him to do something about it if he was who he said he was. They did everything under the sun to get a reaction out of him, but if you check out his life, you will see that the only thing that got him mad was when people offended the Father by misusing his temple (see the Gospel of Matthew, chapter 21, verse 12). The people misusing the temple weren't calling *him* names or punishing *him* unfairly; they were sinning against God, and he couldn't stand for it.

Just like Christ, you have a right to be offended when someone insults, abuses, curses, denies, or slams, in any way, your heavenly Father. More than a right, you have an *obligation* to take offense. But if you wish to imitate Christ, you don't have that same right when it comes to yourself.

Think about this: People can slam you all day and call you what they will, and all the arguing in the world won't change them. And what do you care if it does? Are you now trying to please man, or God? If you are trying to please man, you are no longer pleasing God (see Galatians 1:10). Your goal is to honor your Father, to care more about him and what he says about you than about what they say. But part of honoring your Father is standing up for him. So if someone is offending the Father (sinning against him), then you have every right and, in fact, a duty to stand up to them. It's a fight for your God, not for yourself, because it isn't about you; it's all about him.

It's like this: Whenever I hear someone use the name of Jesus in vain, I get really offended. Not because it offends me personally (note: making me uncomfortable or mad is not a sin) but because it is an offense to him. It is an insult, a slam, a curse, and that makes me mad for him. But I also know that my wrath is nothing like the wrath Jesus showed when he threw over the money changers' tables. I don't have the power he had, but I do have his Word, and that's the next best thing to having him there in the flesh. So this is what I say: "Oh, I wouldn't do that if I were you—use Jesus' name as a cuss word. The Bible says it's a terrible thing to fall into the hands of the living God.** Be careful, I wouldn't

"To this you were called, because Christ suffered for you, leaving you an example, that **you should follow in his steps.** 'He committed no sin, and no deceit was found in his mouth.' When they hurled their insults at him, he did not retaliate; when he suffered, he made no threats. Instead, he entrusted himself to him who judges justly."

—the 1st book of Peter, chapter 2, verses 21–23

** see Hebrews chapter 10, verse 31

97

want to insult God if it were me." Then I do something like shiver in fear and say, "Oooh, not a good thing."

I can't sit by idly while my God is insulted, but I can sit by while I am insulted, just like Christ did when he was hung on that cross. Not once did he fight back. Not once did he argue for himself (Luke 23:9). Instead he trusted the Father to prove him right in the end, and boy, did he ever. So trust God with your reputation. Fight for his. And rest in the fact that "in all things God works for the good of those who love him" (Romans 8:28). And your only job is to ignore it, or as Jesus himself says, "turn the other cheek" (see Matthew 5:39).

Get Over Yourself

Your goal is to get rid of your Mean Girl, but God's goal might be to purify you. Either way, one question that must be looked at when faced with a Mean Girl or any other mean person is, "Will a part of me die because of her?" And the answer must be "yes."

Death seems like such an awful and painful thing, and it can be both of those, but it is also a beautiful and necessary thing in the life of the believer. A symbolic death is on the lips of the apostle Paul when he says, "Those who belong to Christ Jesus have nailed the passions and desires of their sinful nature to his cross and crucified them there" (Galatians 5:24 NLT) and, "So put to death the sinful, earthly things lurking within you" (Colossians 3:5 NLT). This death, this getting over yourself and nailing sin to the cross, is a thing of faith. As the Christ himself said, "I tell you the truth, unless a kernel of wheat falls to the ground and dies, it remains only a single seed. But if it dies, it produces many seeds. The man who loves his life will lose it, while the man who hates his life in this world will keep it for eternal life" (John 12:24–25).

> "If I had cherished sin in my heart, the Lord would not have listened."
> **—King David**
> (Read the book of Psalms, chapter 66, verse 18.)

Every believer is required to take a step toward death—the killing of your sinful nature, that part of you that hates, whines, complains, fears, and so much more. If you don't grasp this concept and begin to desire to put to death that part of you that is inconsistent with holiness, then the Mean Girl in your life will have won. The truth is that your reaction to her is being judged by your God. You are being called on the mat. Will you respond with holiness or cattiness? You see, "when you follow the desires of your sinful nature, your lives will produce these evil results: sexual immorality, impure thoughts, eagerness for lustful pleasure, idolatry, participation in demonic activities, hostility, quarreling, jealousy, outbursts of anger, selfish ambition, divisions, the feeling that everyone is wrong except those in your own little group, envy, drunkenness, wild parties, and other kinds of sin. Let me tell you again, as I have before, that anyone living that sort of life will not inherit the Kingdom of God" (Galatians 5:19–21 NLT). God is watching and he is judging. People talk a lot about grace in the church, but not as much is said about obedience to God's law. Don't make a mockery of his grace by refusing to obey his law; grace doesn't allow you to ignore God's commands. "Make every effort to live in peace with all men and to be holy; without holiness no one will see the Lord" (Hebrews 12:14). See, obedience requires effort, not just a reliance on grace. And there's the danger for you. If you allow the Mean Girl to drag you into her meanness and you choose to disobey the Father, tell me where exactly you see yourself becoming like Christ? Is she worth it? You can see that sin and your Father are not compatible. He asks you to run from it and to kill that part of your nature that craves it.

But how do I do all that? you ask. It goes like this: When you allowed Christ into your heart and made him Lord of your life, a funny thing happened. Sin lost its power over you. You might think it's impossible to stop the cycle of mean in your life, but don't miss this:

So you should consider yourselves dead to sin and able to live for the glory of God through Christ Jesus. Do not let sin control the way you live; do not give in to its lustful desires. Do not let any part of your body become a tool of wickedness, to be used for sinning. Instead, give yourselves completely to God since you have been given new life. And use your whole body as a tool to do what is right for the glory of God. Sin is no longer your master, for you are no longer subject to the law, which enslaves you to sin. Instead, you are free by God's grace.

Romans 6:11–14 NLT

Did you see it? *Sin is no longer your master because of grace.* There it is again. But listen carefully. This grace we speak of doesn't mean you have a free ride to sin all you want and then to be forgiven—don't toy with God like that. Grace means that God has gifted you with the ability to say no to sin. It is no longer your master. So each time you say, "I just can't control myself," remember that's not true anymore. Before you knew God it might have been true, but now it's not. You can and you shall control yourself. But how? How do you die to self? How do you crucify the sin in you? These things sound impossible. But they aren't as impossible as they sound; they are just new concepts that aren't taught at school or sometimes even at church. So what does it mean?

> If God is anything, then He must be everything. And unless He is everything, He is nothing.
> —Dick Woodward

Dying to self means that you stop demanding the world revolve around you.

Dying to self means that you give up the right to always be right.

Dying to self means that you turn the other cheek when someone attacks you and that you do all you can to live in peace, even if it means getting the raw end of the deal.

Dying to self means that all that is in you that isn't holiness and faith has to be denied.

But again, you say, *how*?

1. Call it sin. The first thing you need to do is to identify what part of you needs to die, the sin part. What part of you has to be turned off, said no to, avoided, and even hated? These are the things that violate your spirit. These are the things that you could not tackle without God's grace. In other words, if you claim God's grace, put it to good use and tackle these things that up to now have controlled you. Agree with God that this stuff is sin, call it sin, and get busy getting rid of it, by God's grace.

Following is a list of reactions to Mean Girls that can derail a life of faith in an instant. Each one is followed by a verse reference so you can see it for yourself. God is very clear on what kinds of things drive you from his presence and damage your spirit. Know this list and avoid these things, even when it comes to your Mean Girl.

Fighting

Hostility—Galatians 5:19–21

Quarreling—Galatians 5:19–21

Anger—Colossians 3:5–10

Rage—Colossians 3:5–10

Malicious behavior—Colossians 3:5–10

Outbursts of anger—Galatians 5:19–21

Factions—Galatians 5:19–21

Divisions—Galatians 5:19–21

Feeling everyone is wrong but you—Galatians 5:19–21

Always needing to be right—Galatians 5:26

Irritation with others—Galatians 5:26

Unforgiveness—Matthew 6:14–15

Keeping track of wrongs—1 Corinthians 13:5

Rejoicing when others are wrong—1 Corinthians 13:6

Foolish Talk

Complaining—Philippians 2:14; James 5:9

Foolish talk—Ephesians 5:1–4

Criticizing—Romans 2:1; 14:3

Passing judgment—Romans 3:3

Slander—Colossians 3:8

Dirty language—Colossians 3:8

Lying—Colossians 3:9

Selfishness

Conceit—Galatians 5:26

Selfishness—Galatians 5:19–21

Pride—Proverbs 18:12

Greed—Colossians 3:5

Idolatry—Colossians 3:5

Envy—Proverbs 14:30

Not Trusting Love

Giving up on love—1 Corinthians 13:4

Not trusting—1 Corinthians 13:7

Jealousy—Galatians 5:26

Fear—Isaiah 8:13

Unless you can die to those urges inside you for revenge, hate, and all the other things you allow Mean Girls to instill in you, your faith will be incomplete. Not only incomplete but disobedient, in fact. In his 1st letter to the Thessalonians, Paul writes,

"God has called us to be holy, not to live impure lives. Anyone who refuses to live by these rules is not disobeying human rules but is rejecting God, who gives his Holy Spirit to you" (1 Thessalonians 4:7–8 NLT).

2. Use the Mean Girl. The Mean Girl is your chance to learn to die to self. Really this means you're letting God use the Mean Girl. It's like this: When God asks you to die to self, the dying will be in something that you have to give up—something that you want to do, say, or be. It won't be giving up something that you *don't* want. God's not going to ask you to give up liver and onions if you don't want them in the first place. What would that prove? But if you really love getting revenge, he *is* going to ask you to give that up. Dying to self never involves doing something that's easy to do but always involves something that's a challenge. So don't shrink away from the Mean Girl as an obstacle in your path, but see her as your opportunity to learn more about dying to self.

"If your faith isn't changing you, it hasn't saved you."
—James MacDonald

3. Remember why you die. Every time you die to self, you are getting closer and closer to God. It's like lifting weights—each time it hurts, you grow stronger and stronger. Remember that each time you hurt by reacting in a holy way, you become more and more like Christ. "For what credit is it if, when you sin and are beaten for it, you endure? But if when you do good and suffer for it you endure, this is a gracious thing in the sight of God. For to this you have been called, because Christ also suffered for you, leaving you an example, so that you might fol-

"Since therefore Christ suffered in the flesh, arm yourselves with the same way of thinking, for whoever has suffered in the flesh has ceased from sin, so as to live for the rest of the time in the flesh no longer for human passions but for the will of God."
—1 Peter 4:1–2 ESV

low in his steps" (1 Peter 2:20–21 ESV). If you can remember that the goal is holiness, then each time you deny your urges, you will feel a life of faith growing in you.

4. Be strong. When you practice dying to self, you will find that you actually become a stronger and better believer.* You don't really die at all. Only the bad parts of you die. It's true, "everyone who exalts himself will be humbled, and he who humbles himself will be exalted" (quoting Jesus in Luke chapter 14, verse 11 ESV). But I also want you to be careful not to use this message to belittle yourself or to consider yourself unimportant. Turn to *Standing Up to the Mean Girl*, page 108, to find out more about being an assertive, self-respecting girl.

The next time you scream at God, **"Why me? Why this Mean Girl** in my life?" **think about this:** His Word doesn't answer why *this* particular girl is in your life on *this* particular day, but it does tell you that you are called to a life of obedience. And that means obedience not just when obedience is easy but when it's the hardest thing you have ever done.

Hannah Sees the Truth

Lately, my Father has revealed to me a depth of selfishness in myself that I never even so much as suspected. I find that all my kindness to others, my benevolence, and what seemed to be the most unselfish acts of my life, all have had their root in a deep and subtle form of self-love. My motto has for a long time been "Freely you have received, freely give" and I dreamed that in a certain sense I was living up to it, not only as regards physical blessings, but spiritual as well.

But I find now that I have never really given one thing freely in my life. I have always expected and demanded pay of some kind for every gift, and where the pay has failed to come, the gifts have invariably ceased to flow. If I gave love, I demanded love

*"Stressed-out grumblers are two-and-a-half times more susceptible to colds than grateful people." —Brennan Manning

in return; if I gave kindness, I demanded gratitude as payment; if I gave counsel, I demanded obedience to it, or if not that, at least an increase of respect for my judgment on the part of the one counseled; if I gave the gospel, I demanded conversions or a reputation of zeal and holiness; if I gave consideration, I demanded consideration in return. In short I sold everything and gave nothing. I know nothing of the meaning of Christ's words "Freely you have received, freely give." But I did it ignorantly.

Now, however, the Lord has opened my eyes to see something of the nature and extent of this selfishness, and I believe He is also giving me grace to overcome it in a measure. I have been taking home to myself the lesson contained in Matt. 5:39–48. I desire to do everything now as to the Lord alone, and to receive my pay only from Him. His grace must carry on this work in me for I am utterly powerless to do one thing toward it; but I feel assured that He will.

And I feel I have to thank Him for what He has already done. He has conquered a feeling of repugnance which was growing in me towards someone with whom I am brought into very close contact, and enabled me to give freely, without even wanting any return. Oh how great He is in strength and wisdom!

—Hannah*

Obstinacy and self-will will always **stab Jesus Christ.** It may hurt no one else, but it **wounds His Spirit.** Whenever we are obstinate and self-willed and set upon our own ambitions, we are **hurting Jesus**. Every time we stand on our rights and insist that this is what we intend to do, we are **persecuting Jesus**. Whenever we stand on our dignity we systematically vex and **grieve His Spirit**; and when the knowledge comes home that it is Jesus Whom we have been persecuting all the time, it is the most crushing revelation there could be.

Is the word of God tremendously keen to me as I hand it on to you, or does my life give the lie to the things I profess to teach? I may teach sanctification and yet exhibit the spirit of Satan, the spirit that persecutes Jesus Christ. The Spirit of Jesus is conscious of one thing only—a perfect oneness with the Father, and He says, "Learn of Me, for I am meek and lowly in heart." All I do ought to be founded on a perfect oneness with Him, not on a self-willed determination to be godly. This will mean that I can be easily put upon, easily over-reached, easily ignored; but if I submit to it for His sake, I prevent Jesus Christ being persecuted.

—Oswald Chambers, *My Utmost for His Highest*

Standing Up to the Mean Girl

Standing up to the Mean Girl is not getting in her face. It's not arguing back or attacking. That's not standing up to her. Standing up in the face of attack is simply removing yourself from the attack, either by saying something or by just walking off. Standing up to a Mean Girl is really standing up for your promise to please God over self. If you get in her face to fight for yourself, you lose sight of God because her face obscures your view, but if you stand up to her in order to please God, he is between you and her, and he is still your focus. So when you stand up to her, be sure that you are doing it to please God, not yourself.

While you live in the land of Mean Girls, I want you to understand that you aren't the victim; you are the faithful one. You aren't their prey; you are a lover of enemies. When you can see yourself as a tool in the hands of God rather than a target in the eyes of the Mean Girl, you win.

Before you get out there and start standing up, you've gotta note one more subtlety: How you talk to a believer and how you talk to a non-believer are really different. They are not coming from the same place, so you need to approach them according to different standards. Let's break it down.

> "The LORD your God is with you, he is mighty to save. He will take great delight in you, he will quiet you with his love, he will rejoice over you with singing."
>
> —the prophet Zephaniah, from the book of Zephaniah, chapter 3, verse 17

See *The Battle Isn't against Flesh and Blood*, page 174, on standing firm.

Standing Up to Non-Believers

Non-believers are a different animal than believers simply because they don't live according to God's law. Therefore they can't be confronted with God's law, because it will mean nothing to them. As believers we aren't to be surprised by the cruel acts of non-believers; they do them because they are unrepentant, refusing to live by God's law. So know that if you attempt to confront them with "sin," you will be throwing pearls after swine, because they won't understand you. Instead you are to follow the precepts of loving your enemy. And remember, love isn't a feeling, because a feeling cannot be commanded, and love is commanded. Therefore love is simply an action that we do no matter how we feel.

If you feel compelled to stand up to a mean non-believer, know that it probably won't change her, but it will let her know that you aren't an easy target. As I've said before, if you don't cave and get all freaked out, then she is less interested. Here's an example: If she is calling you a slut and threatening to tell your boyfriend some big lie, you can say something like, "Okay, that's fine. If he's truly a smart guy, he won't believe you. Do whatever you like," and then leave. Remember, you aren't sent by God to call her on the carpet for her sin when she is unaware of what sin is. Convicting her is the job of the Holy Spirit (1 Corinthians 5:9–13; John 16:8). But you can stand strong by letting her know that you won't be her victim or pawn by simply not breaking under her pressure. Remember that it doesn't matter what she says or thinks, only what God says and thinks.

Standing up often means not giving in to her attempt to make you mad and not giving in to your urge to get even. Standing up means standing on your faith that all of this is okay and under God's control. It also can mean refusing to be manipulated or made scared by her. Standing up can be many things, but, I repeat, it is never violent, hateful, confrontational, or hurtful. Standing up is simply being aware of who you are and making sure she knows you don't need her approval or love to be whole. It's confidence in your faith and your God.

Standing Up to Believers

Believers, on the other hand, are held to a higher standard by God, and therefore you can talk to them of God's commands such as love and kindness. But as I will say several times in this section, that's not always the option God wants for you at the time. For one thing, it is important that we, as believers, hold one another accountable, but it also important that we understand that some girls who call themselves believers might actually be lying to themselves and to you. In that case, whatever you say about faith might fall on deaf ears, so don't be surprised. But if she is a true believer who really wants to serve God, then hearing from you might be just the thing she needs to turn her life around.

RECONCILIATION

God's Word talks about only two times when you might go to a sister in Christ who's shown she has something against you or against God's call to love you. One is in Matthew chapter 5, verses 23 and 24.

> If you are offering your gift at the altar and there remember that your ~~brother~~ *mean girl* has something against you, leave your gift there in front of the altar. First go and be reconciled to your ~~brother~~ *mean girl*, then come and offer your gift.

In this instance notice that Jesus tells you that if she has something against *you*, you should go and work it out. If your Mean Girl is a believer, it is up to you to go to her with the issue. This might mean apologizing for what makes her mad or loving her in spite of her attitude. It doesn't mean pointing your finger at her, getting in her face, calling her a name, or trying to fix her. This isn't permission to be holier-than-thou. It's a call to love one another and not let problems ruin friendships. So only pull this verse on a sister in Christ. Only use it when you know that you can do something to help the situation—that is, to have reconciliation. (Note: The word *reconcile* means to restore to friendship or harmony. So whatever harmonious or good relationship you had before she got mad at you is the relationship you try to get back to. You might think about the fact that if she was never your friend to start with, you can't expect to be restored to a great friendship, because you can't restore what you never had.)

CONFRONTATION

If another believer sins against you, go privately and point out the fault. If the other person listens and confesses it, you have won that person back. But if you are unsuccessful, take one or two others with you and go back again, so that everything you say may be confirmed by two or three witnesses. If that person still refuses to listen, take your case to the church. If the church decides you are right, but the other person won't accept it, treat that person as a pagan or a corrupt tax collector.

Matthew 18:15–17 NLT

This was a Jewish custom. When someone sinned against God and a believer was aware of his sin, he was to confront him privately. It was really an ugly embarrassment as well as a sin to bring other people into the situation unless it got really out of hand. The godly thing to do was to first talk to the person privately, not to punish him but to help bring him back to a right relationship with God. The translation of "sins against you" was more than likely not part of the original text but is meant to get across the idea that someone sins against God by doing something to you. Their real sin is always against God but oftentimes perpetrated on you. That's part of the reason why you have no right to revenge. It's God's job, remember, to punish and judge. If the sinning person didn't see the error of his ways then, Jesus said, you should take one or two other people who knew of the sin as well and confront the person to bring him to repentance. Then, if he still refused to admit he had done anything sinful, the church should be brought in to do a kind of intervention, confronting him with his sin and hoping to finally jolt him into seeing the reality of his ways. In the end, if the person was still numb to his sinfulness, he was to be kicked out of the church—again, in the hope that this would really knock some sense into him.

Now before we go any further, let me throw out a major note of caution. I mention this verse because I want you to know Scripture, but when I was your age I found it very hard to separate my emotions from the problem. And if I had taken this verse as a call to action, I would have ended up making the Mean Girl madder than she was—because if you aren't completely emotionally detached, you're gonna come off as holier-than-thou and just using God's Word to get revenge.

Hayley's Hint #7: Never use the Word of God to manipulate or get even with people.

This verse is tricky, and a lot of people use it too cavalierly. Be very careful that you're sure God is calling you to take this girl to the mat spiritually. Be sure that you aren't being overly judgmental or sensitive. This verse is for real sin that *must* be confronted, so tread lightly here. Remember, you are called to turn the other cheek. If you obsess about teaching her a lesson or proving her wrong and your motives are impure, then beware, God will not be pleased. This is why I suggest that your first reaction should be to ignore her attack and love her. You don't know where she is in her faith, and you can't be sure that she even chooses to live by faith, so use this verse only in rare situations. If you use it every time you feel slighted, you will begin to abuse it, and you will find that the attacks will be even stronger and the name-calling will turn toward your holier-than-thou behavior. Talk to God before you attempt to use this verse. Ask him if his call to you is to die to self rather than to cure the Mean Girl. Ask him, "Is what she did a sin?" Does he call what she is doing a sin? If you think that she has sinned against the Father, how would he have you remind her? Is confrontation a good idea? What verses in the Bible say that she has sinned against God? Be sure you are on solid footing before you go to her about what seems to be a sin.

Verse Note: This is a verse on church discipline. How many times have you seen this done in your church? If mature Christians are not using this at every drop of the hat, then you'd better check yourself. It isn't something to be taken lightly. So tread carefully.

THE HOW-TO'S

Now if you still feel compelled to say something, you should do it when she is alone, so she doesn't get embarrassed in front of her friends. Also remember to do it in love, not judging or condemning her and not telling her what she did to *you*. Take yourself out of the equation. If you can't take yourself out of the equation because you are upset, then wait until you can. And finally, remember, your job is not to change her or punish her, just to remind her of God's law and her trespasses against it. She might not really have realized what she is doing. When she does, she might ask for forgiveness right away, but don't demand that in response to your following God's law. Your job is to obey him, not to demand that she does as well.

Check yourself: If you think it's a serious sin against God, then think about testing your situation with a neutral adult (i.e., not your parent) who can shed light on things and see whether your motives are pure before you bring this up to the Mean Girl.

(Note: Don't have the adult do it for you. Just have them check you.) They can keep you from being distracted from the more likely response you might be being called to give—forgiveness and grace.

I know I have given you a lot of "be carefuls" and "check yourselfs" in this chapter, but when it comes to standing up, you really do need to do those things. Standing up is to be used in rare instances, because most of the time turning the other cheek is more appropriate. In everything that you do, make sure that your motives are pure and that you are only doing what his Word, not your emotions, calls you to do.

God's Plan for Your Mean Girl

If the Mean Girl is your enemy, then God's plan for her and you is simple. It's called love. All over this book we've been talking about love, specifically loving your enemies. And you've probably been scratching your head and saying, "How? I don't feel anything but hate for her. How can I love her? I don't even like her."

In lots of places in Scripture, God commands us to love:

- **"Love the LORD your God with all your heart and with all your soul and with all your strength" (Deuteronomy 6:5).**
- **"Love your neighbor as yourself" (Matthew 22:39).**
- **"Love your enemies, do good to those who hate you" (Luke 6:27).**

Each one of those is a command. If love were a feeling first, then could it be commanded? For example, could someone command you to feel frustrated? Or happy? Or sad even? Let me answer that for you: No. Feelings can't be commanded, so since the Bible commands us to love, love can't be a feeling. When God commands us to love, he wants us to take action in spite of what we are feeling. If you think about it, this makes total sense. If God wanted you to wait till you *felt* love, then love would become all about you. It would be a self-centered kind of thing, like "I will only love you if you make me feel good." But that's where the world gets it wrong. Love isn't about how you feel. We aren't called to love to get something out of it; we are called to love so *someone else* gets something out of it.

Love = Giving

So what is love if it isn't a feeling? Another stellar question. In order to understand love, let's look at love himself and see how he operates. Of course I am talking about God, for "God is love" (1 John 4:8).

> For **God so loved the world** that he gave his one and only Son, that whoever believes in him shall not perish but have eternal life.
>
> John 3:16
>
> I live by faith in the **Son of God,** who **loved me** and gave himself for me.
>
> Galatians 2:20

Do you see the pattern? God loved, so God gave. Love is first born in giving. Giving is about caring for the other person and giving them what they need for faith and life. "God so loved the world." Notice it doesn't say, "the world made God feel so good that he loved it." Again, not to beat a dead pony, but love isn't about feeling good. God set an example for us in his love. And the life of Christ that we as believers seek to imitate is a clear example of love. Do you really think that Christ was overcome with love and joy as he was being whipped and nailed to a cross? Love is about giving, not getting. Love is about caring, not being cared for. Love is about helping, not being helped. Love reaches outside itself and gives to others. Love isn't concerned with self; it is concerned with others. The love that God commands is pure, holy, and untainted by self-gratification.

A girl once asked me, "Isn't it hypocritical to do nice things for people when you don't feel like it, when you don't even like them?" According to the world, yes, but hypocrisy isn't about feelings any more than love is. You don't judge a hypocrite based on whether they felt like doing what they did or not; you judge based on whether they did what they believe or not. Doing what God calls you to do is never hypocrisy, even when you don't feel like it. A hypocrite is a person who doesn't do what God calls them to do when they believe that his commands are good and should be followed. Or when someone tells others that trusting God is good but fails to do it themselves—that is being a hypocrite. Let's face it, we are called to do what God commands whether we like it or not, and love is no different. You do it because he tells you to. Feelings are off the table.

It's like this: Every day I get up and go to work. Some days I don't feel like getting out of bed, let alone getting dressed and going to work, but I do anyway. Does that make me a hypocrite? No, doing what you have to do even when you don't feel like it is never hypocrisy. It is *integrity*. So it won't make you a hypocrite to give love when you don't feel loving.

Love Is . . .

Love is an amazing thing. It's more than we ever imagined and more than we ever thought we could do. But remember, girls, that God never asks us to do what we cannot do. He gives us all we need to follow his commands—even the command to love our enemies. I know it seems impossible, but take heart! You don't have to like her to love her. You don't even have to feel anything good toward her at all to love her. All you have to do is want to please God. If you love him, that's enough to love anybody—mean, nice, or in-between.

Mean Girl Love

What I want you to understand from all this is that you don't give love in order to get what you want. Ever. That's where hypocrisy lies. Love isn't about getting something out of it. Not even with the Mean Girl. I've told you several times already that if you obey God and love the Mean Girl, you might find that you've won her over or at least stopped her attacks. But let me tell you this: Your obedience to God should never be for selfish reasons. Don't follow him to get things. And don't obey his command to love in order to get something in return. Your goal in loving the Mean Girl is not to get her to change. Your goal is to honor God by loving your enemies. A wonderful side effect of obeying God might just be that she stops picking on you, but that isn't your concern when you are loving God's way. Her change is in his hands, and it can't be your main goal. It is simply a by-product of faith.

"I do not like to think of you as **needing** to have 'things' pleasant around you when you **have God** within you.

Surely He is **enough** to content any soul. **If** He is **not** enough here, how will it be in the future life **when** we have only Him Himself?"

—Hannah Whitall Smith

What's Love Got to Do with It?

To better understand how to give this love that God commands, let's take another walk through the Scriptures. In *The Message*, author Eugene Peterson describes God's love like this:

Love never gives up.

Love cares more for others than for self.
Love doesn't want what it doesn't have.
Love doesn't strut,
Doesn't have a swelled head,
Doesn't force itself on others,

Isn't always "me first,"

Doesn't fly off the handle,

Doesn't keep score of the sins of others,

Doesn't revel when others grovel,
Takes pleasure in the flowering of truth,

Puts up with anything,
Trusts God always,

Always looks for the best,
Never looks back,
But keeps going to the end.
Love never dies.

1 Corinthians 13:4–8 MESSAGE

Jesus on Mean Girls

Mean Girls aren't a shock to Jesus. They aren't anything new. They existed when he walked the earth, before he walked the earth, and after he left the earth. And I would bet that they will be here long after you leave the earth. Mean Girls exist, and you can't do anything about that without the Word of God in your head and heart. So what does Jesus say about Mean Girls? How does following him make a difference?

The book *Hinds' Feet on High Places* by Hannah Hurnard tells a great story about following Jesus even when it seems ridiculous. In this great little book, a young girl named Much Afraid lives her life in fear. When the Shepherd offers to take her away from the land of fearing and up to the high places, she fearfully agrees. During her journey she is tested to her limits, and on one of those occasions her relatives catch up with her and attack her with doubts about the Shepherd who is leading her. As they throw lies at Much Afraid, they tell her that the Shepherd is deceiving her. He is leading her astray, *down* the mountain rather than *up* the mountain. How can that get her to the high places? As she looks around she sees that it is true. They are going down, not up, and for a moment she starts to think that maybe the Shepherd *is* lying to her. When she asks the Shepherd to explain himself and his apparent deception, he asks her a question: *"Would you be willing to trust me even if everything in the wide world seemed to say that I was deceiving you—indeed, that I had deceived you all along?"*

What a question. It made me cry as I read it. Would *I* trust him even if everything in the world said he was lying? *Could I do it?* I sobbed. The thought was frightening, but then, just as quickly as Much Afraid, I made my decision. She said,

> "Yes, I'm sure I would, because one thing I know to be true, it is impossible that you should deceive me. I know that I am often very frightened at the things which you ask me to do," she added

shamefacedly and apologetically, "but I could never doubt you in that way. It's myself I am afraid of, never of you, and though everyone in the world should tell me that you had deceived me, I should know it was impossible."*

What a thing to say. To the world it sounds insane. Incredible. Naive. But to a believer it sounds natural. We follow Christ because we believe him—all of him, all the time. Not just when it makes sense, and not just when it's easy. That's for the half-hearted Christian, the lukewarm one who gets spit out of his mouth (see Revelation 3:16). But for those of us who want to stand the test of time, for those of us who want to rise to new heights and scale new mountains, it's natural. My one passion in life is to please him, and though I fail over and over again, I know that it is a noble mission. And as part of that mission I know that I will have to believe and, yes, even do things that might seem the opposite of sane. Some things he's going to ask me to do will be "insane." They will seem like just plain bad advice, but I will follow it anyway. Why? Because of the One who gives it.

If you too want to follow the leading of your Christ, if you want to be faithful when your faith is put to the test, then let's start now. Let's try to figure out how he tells us to treat Mean Girls. Let's dissect his words and see if we can't make them make sense to our feeble little minds.

In Luke 6, after Jesus had just given his disciples and a crowd of people the Beatitudes, he went up to a quieter place to talk to his disciples, and there he told them about Mean Girls. Well, not exactly about Mean *Girls* but about mean people, of which girls are some. In fact, Jesus told them about all people, including people you don't like and people who are your enemies. And this is what he said:

> But if you are willing to listen, I say, love your enemies. Do good to those who hate you. Pray for the happiness of those

*Hannah Hurnard, *Hinds' Feet on High Places*, page 168

who curse you. Pray for those who hurt you. If someone slaps you on one cheek, turn the other cheek. If someone demands your coat, offer your shirt also. Give what you have to anyone who asks you for it; and when things are taken away from you, don't try to get them back. Do for others as you would like them to do for you.

Luke 6:27–31 NLT

Now, I know I've already given you this verse, but let's look at it more closely this time. This is what Jesus is saying in a nutshell:

1. Love girls you don't like. (Love your enemies.)
2. Do good to girls who don't like you. (Do good to those who hate you.)
3. Pray for the girls who slam you. (Pray for the happiness of those who curse you.)
4. Pray for those who are mean to you. (Pray for those who hurt you.)
5. Don't get even. (If someone slaps you on one cheek, turn to him the other also.)
6. Give, give, give till it hurts. (Give what you have to anyone who asks you for it; and when things are taken away from you, don't try to get them back.)
7. Treat others like you want to be treated. (Do for others as you would like them to do for you.)

Jesus is talking about his kind of love here: unconditional and not a feeling but an action. That's the kind of love we all want to get—to be loved by someone no matter what you do wrong, or how you hurt them, or how they might feel at the time. It's the love that God has for his children. It's not about what they do wrong or right. No, it's just about the fact that they have been adopted as daughters of the Father, and that's that, period. So Jesus was teaching his disciples to love like the

Father does. Unconditionally. Now that seems really romantic when you are talking about your boyfriend. Of course you want him to love you unconditionally. You even want your parents to do that. It's a beautiful thing when you receive it, but did you know that he also wants *you* to give your enemies the same kind of love?

> If you want to know the true character of a person, then watch how they treat people who can do nothing for them—or better yet, watch how they treat their enemies. That will show you their true character.

It's a weak faith that only loves the one who loves them back. I always say that if you want to know the true character of a person, then watch how they treat people who can do nothing for them—or better yet, watch how they treat their enemies. As you watch their behavior, you will see who they really are, because when the rubber hits the road, that's when the true you comes out. And that's why Jesus says that we are supposed to love our enemies like this. He wants your true character, that same character he has, to be seen in you.

So if Jesus is giving us a blueprint for our character, let's look to see how it applies to our lives. Right here in your book, write down the names of the girls in your school who are mean. Write down at least one girl who is hurting you or trying to control you.

_____

_____

_____

Now turn the page, and this time put these same names in the blanks. This is your to-do list from God. This is how you are to handle the Mean Girl.

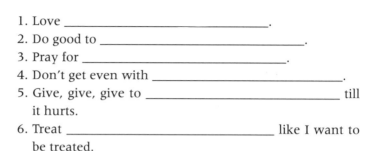

1. Love _____.
2. Do good to _____.
3. Pray for _____.
4. Don't get even with _____.
5. Give, give, give to _____ till it hurts.
6. Treat _____ like I want to be treated.

Now take a look at this list. Can you imagine doing all those things? Does it seem possible for you to agree with God's Word when it comes to the Mean Girl? Hard, I have to admit. As I look at it myself, I think, "O Lord, I don't know how to do this." And he says, "Good, that's why I'm here. If it were easy, then it wouldn't be faith." See, the commands of God come with help. God's help. "For it is God who works in you to will and to act according to his good purpose" (Philippians 2:13).

As you attempt to understand the Mean Girl, you can start to understand yourself. What if the Mean Girl exists only to give you a way to prove to God that you will follow him no matter what? What if she is your refiner's fire, the trial made to purify you and make you holy? Will you allow God to do with you what he wants, or will you let her shape you into the image of her? "God created people in his own image; God patterned them after himself; male and female he created them" (Genesis 1:27 NLT). Whose image will you be made in?

Jesus goes on in Luke 6:32–34 (NLT):

Do you think you deserve credit merely for loving those who love you? Even the sinners do that! And if you do good only to those who do good to you, is that so wonderful? Even sinners do that much! And if you lend money only to those who can repay you, what good is that? Even sinners will lend to their own kind for a full return.

In this part Jesus talks about cutting corners: taking God's Word and only using it when it's easy. That's the point here—if you only treat them well when it's easy, then what good is it? Even bad people do that. Mean people love the people who love them, and they lend stuff out if they know they'll get it back. They do all these things because it's safe for them. It makes sense. But God's law doesn't make sense. "For the message of the cross is foolishness to those who are perishing, but to us who are being saved it is the power of God" (1 Corinthians 1:18). It's sheer stupidity to those who don't believe. But for those of us who do, it might seem stupid to us sometimes, but we follow it anyway.

So if you say, "I am loving and kind, I pray for people, and I don't get even," well, good. But the question is, are you the same way with girls who are hurting you? Are you the same faithful person to your enemies? After all, it isn't anything big to love people who love you back; that isn't faith, that's common sense. But you are called to a higher understanding, one of faith that says God's law is my law. I will follow it even if it costs me. After all, it's hard to appreciate things that don't cost you anything. What is more valuable to you, a car you saved 3 years to buy, or a hand-me-down car from your parents? Things of cost are of great value. And your faith, to be of great value, will need to be of great cost.

Are you willing to sit at Jesus' feet and listen to his words on Mean Girls? If so, here is God's call for you:

Love your enemies! Do good to them! Lend to them! And don't be concerned that they might not repay. Then your reward from heaven will be very great, and you will truly be acting as children of the Most High, for he is kind to the

You don't know what it means to believe until you have to believe.

unthankful and to those who are wicked. You must be compassionate, just as your Father is compassionate. Stop judging others, and you will not be judged. Stop criticizing others, or it will all come back on you. If you forgive others, you will be forgiven. If you give, you will receive. Your gift will return to you in full measure, pressed down, shaken together to make room for more, and running over. Whatever measure you use in giving—large or small—it will be used to measure what is given back to you.

Luke 6:35–38 NLT

And just for one more kick in the butt, here are some of the same verses summed up in Eugene Peterson's paraphrase of the Bible, *The Message*:

Don't pick on people, jump on their failures, criticize their faults—unless, of course, you want the same treatment. Don't condemn those who are down; that hardness can boomerang. Be easy on people; you'll find life a lot easier. Give away your life; you'll find life given back, but not merely given back—given back with bonus and blessing. Giving, not getting, is the way. Generosity begets generosity.

Luke 6:37–38 MESSAGE

When

people live according to

humanity's ideas

and not

according to God,

they are like the devil.

—**Augustine**

Boys and Your Mean Girl

In my book *Dateable*, the topic of girls lying to themselves was a biggie. (If you haven't read *Dateable*, I suggest you find yourself a copy and give it a gander.) Remember? Girls lying to themselves is like an epidemic. We all do it, and we all pay the price for it. And one of our biggest lies, which totally destroys relationships, is the lie that it's the other girl's fault. Sound familiar? If a girl is flirting with your boyfriend and he seems to like it, you go after her with all claws out. How dare she get into your territory, I mean, she knew you two were dating! And the fight's on. Your goal becomes to get even with that chick. Meanwhile the guy might get some kind of relationship time-out where you punish him a little bit but soon take him back after he's had time to think about it. The girl, on the other hand, is archenemy number one for eternity. You certainly couldn't ever trust her again. Look what she did!

Okay, let me interrupt your tantrum as you stomp your feet and say, "That's right, it's her fault!" Do you see the problem here? Two people do something, and you choose to blame only one of them because she's female. Your first thought is that if there's a bad person involved, it's the girl. I know the feeling. Girls *are* conniving. They pretty much can't be trusted when it comes to guys—but let's not forget that guys pretty much can't be trusted either when it comes to raging hormones and sexual appetites. **So why does the girl get the brunt of your wrath?** Why are catfights so prevalent? What is it about our own gender that makes us so mad?

I believe that every time you fight another girl, **you break down the bond that God meant there to**

> "Be devoted to one another in brotherly *and sisterly* love. Honor one another above yourselves."
>
> —the book of Romans, chapter 12, verse 10

be between girls. And because of this plan of God's, a girlfriend can be one of the most magical and sacred things you can have. She's your support system, your revitalizer, your biggest fan. And she is part of the larger feminine community that you are single-handedly tearing down every time you attack another girl. Did you know that the majority of derogative terms used in name-calling girls are said by *other girls,* not guys?* Then we wonder why girls are considered sluts and guys are just considered studs. Or why girls are considered witches and guys are just considered assertive. It's because of other girls' name-calling, not guys'. Our name-calling just gives guys permission to do the same. Girls are the ones who try to tear down other girls; the guys usually aren't doing it. They're just watching and learning.

Do you realize the importance of how you treat other girls? Do you think that when God calls us to "**love our enemies,**" he is only talking about guys? Or could he mean girls as well? (Check it in Matthew 5:44.) Imagine a world where girls lived this truth, where they embodied loving and caring. God's law makes it clear that love is the ultimate command. So what happens when we revolt against that and decide instead to be the mean, biting, backstabbing, and revengeful ones? Simple—we tear the fabric of femininity. We give us a bad name.

At a high school camp I asked a roomful of boys if they thought that girls were mean, and they all raised their hands. "Girls are mean," one guy said, and they all joined in. "They don't get over things!" another guy chimed. "We fight and then get over it, but girls fight and never forget it. They're crazy!" Don't you hate it when guys say they don't understand girls?

> "For if you forgive men when they sin against you, your heavenly Father will also forgive you. But **if you do not forgive men their sins, your Father will not forgive your sins.**"
> —the Gospel of Matthew, chapter 6, verses 14–15

*9 out of 10 people who call someone a slut are girls (MTV, 5/19/03).

They just can't figure us out. Maybe it's because of this one thing: We don't get over things. I believe that it's a lot harder for girls to live out the verse about loving your enemies than for guys. And that's not natural. Guys tend to be more aggressive and protective, so you'd think they would have a harder time loving their enemies than we do, but it doesn't seem that way. Guys might get mad and fight, but they don't seek to destroy one another. They aren't out to soil the image of the other guy. They work it out and move on.

So what if girls could be that same way? What if as a gender we started, girl by girl, to get over it, especially when it came to our own sex? Do you think we might cause a change in the world? Can you see God smile? If you want to honor your God and follow his law, then one big step is to apply his law to your own sex. Learn how he wants you to love, and remind yourself that this includes girls. Your sisters!

Girls have to stick together. We have to start to forgive more freely and love more

"Don't hit back; discover beauty in everyone. If you've got it in you, get along with everybody. Don't insist on getting even; that's not for you to do. 'I'll do the judging,' says God. 'I'll take care of it.' Our Scriptures tell us that if you see your enemy hungry, go buy that person lunch, or if he's thirsty, get him a drink. Your generosity will surprise him with goodness. Don't let evil get the best of you; get the best of evil by doing good."

—the book of Romans 12:17–21
MESSAGE

honestly. Not in selfishness, only giving when we get back what we want. If Jesus told the truth—and I believe he did—then you have to learn this. If you believe him and want to do what he calls you to do, then you have to stop attacking your sisters. You have to learn to love the feminine gender as much as he does. We are your training ground. We are where the rubber hits the road. We girls are your opportunity to show God that you love him by living out his law in day-to-day life.

If you find yourself in a situation where a girl steals your man, think about it like this: Who do you have a closer relationship with? I hope you say the boyfriend. If he is closest to you, then shouldn't he bear the brunt of guilt for leaving you? Why would you blame the girl? He supposedly loved you more. Don't lie to yourself. If your boyfriend robbed a bank, would you go to the bank and get mad at them for leaving the money lying around for him to take? No, you'd get mad at him. Start telling yourself the truth. Don't blame the girl just because she's a girl. Be honest with yourself and put blame where blame should be. That doesn't mean you never forgive; it just means you realize who you can trust with your heart and who you can't. If your boyfriend has loyalty issues, your problem should be with him, not with the girl. If we can get this right, it will straighten out a lot of the problems with guys and your Mean Girl.

choosing **Beauty** over the Beast

The Girl Grown Up (G.G.U.)

How to Be Mean-Free

If you want to be mean-free, you have to start by checking out yourself and your friends. Are you mean or nice? Are they? This is important because your friends are a reflection of you. Think about this for a minute: "Can two people walk together without agreeing on the direction?" (That's wisdom from the book of Amos, chapter 3, verse 3 NLT.)

So what does this stuff mean to your heart? How can you walk somewhere with someone if you don't agree about where you are going? See, it's a fact of life and, yes, of faith, that you tend to become like the people you hang out with. So it's time for a serious look at your buds. Do you look at them and say, "Yeah, I want to be just like them," or do you look at them and cringe? In order to be the girl grown up you want to be, you need to spend most of your time with other girls grown up. They'll rub off on you, and you can hold each other accountable to goodness.

Let me ask you this. Do you think God smiles when you are mean, or when you are good? If you want to live by his Word, then you have no choice but to drop the mean scene and pick up the good vibe. So check out what makes you mean-free and decide today if that's the kind of life you want.

Note: What is the opposite of the Mean Girl? As I racked my brain to try to figure it out, my first thought was, well, of course, it's the nice girl. But "nice girl" has come to be kind of a bad term, almost an insult. So I kept thinking. Finally I said to myself, a girl grown up is the complete opposite of a Mean Girl. The girl grown up is a good friend. She is obedient to her Father. So from now on, the opposite of the Mean Girl is the G.G.U.

My cry to you, my dear ones, right now, is to decide to be a **Girl Grown Up**. Choose to be godly and good over mean. Be a new, anti-mean girl. If you want to be a good friend and a good girl, then look over this list and start learning and practicing what G.G.U.'s do.

1. *G.G.U.'s aren't defensive.* G.G.U.'s can be confronted with stuff without flipping out. After all, it isn't all about you; it's all about loving the Lord your God with all your heart, soul, and mind and loving your neighbor as yourself. *"Jesus replied, 'You must love the Lord your God with all your heart, all your soul, and all your mind.' This is the first and greatest commandment. A second is equally important: 'Love your neighbor as yourself'"* (Matthew chapter 22, verses 37–39 NLT). If you truly want to grow to be a better person, you'll be open to learning more about yourself. Face it, you're too close to yourself to see where you need, shall we say, improvements. No one can ever see all their own faults; that's why God gave us friends. Just like iron sharpens iron, friends make each other sharper and more useful.

2. *G.G.U.'s don't gossip.* Gossip. God hates it. (See the book of Leviticus, chapter 19, verse 16.) It's yucky. Painful. Vicious. Uncalled-for. G.G.U.'s avoid gossip because God detests it, period, the end. Don't let gossip rule your heart. Just say no.

3. *G.G.U.'s don't seek revenge.* Revenge is a sin. It's taking what's God's. He is the only one with the power of punishment, not you. Don't take over God's role and try to be God in your relationships. Danger. Bad territory to mess around in.

4. *G.G.U.'s are spiritual, not religious.* You have a relationship with a living and breathing being, Jesus Christ, not with a list of laws and regulations. The moment you step away from Christ and into the law is the moment it gets a lot easier to be a Mean Girl.

5. *G.G.U.'s aren't afraid to look stupid.* Who are you trying to please? God or man? If you are trying to please man, you'll freak out if someone sees you do something stupid.

But I believe you would rather please God than man, so don't be afraid to look stupid. It isn't about appearances but who you are. Laugh at yourself. Don't worry about your image as much as loving others.

6. *G.G.U.'s care for others.* If Christ is your example, then check him out. He wasn't all about his needs; he was all about others. He worked when he was tired, and he healed when he was worn out. He gave to others who could do nothing for him. If you care for others, you will never be called a Mean Girl.

7. *G.G.U.'s hold each other accountable.* In the book of Revelation, chapter 2, verses 4, 14, and 20, you will find that Jesus held the church accountable for its actions. As friends, we keep each other in check. A G.G.U. knows that it's healthy to tell each other the truth in love. She isn't afraid to confront her friend and to talk things out.

8. *G.G.U.'s forgive.* Check out 1 Corinthians chapter 13, verse 5. God forgives, therefore good girls forgive. If you want to imitate Christ, forgiveness is your first action item. No forgiveness *from* you, no forgiveness *for* you. *"If you forgive those who sin against you, your heavenly Father will forgive you"* (the book of Matthew, chapter 6, verse 14 NLT).

9. *G.G.U.'s are happy for the wins of their friends.* It doesn't have to be all about you. You want others to be happy, and when they are, you are. G.G.U.'s don't feel bad when other people win, because after all, it isn't all about you.

10. *G.G.U.'s leave others feeling good about themselves.* G.G.U.'s aren't in it for their own glory. They truly care about others, so when they are with people, people feel the love. Don't leave your friends feeling worse than when they started talking to you. Care about them and you will be a true G.G.U.

If you agree with that list and want to start today to live it, then sign the Girl Grown Up Contract at the beginning of the

Ammo for the Battle section, page 189. It's a contract between you and God to be signed in the presence of other sisters in Christ. This is your chance to commit yourself to honoring him no matter what. It's also your chance to take a stand and turn back the tide of Mean Girls. With each girl who signs the contract, we are one girl closer to changing the feminine species from mean to faithful. This is not a contract to take lightly. Heck, it isn't a task to take lightly. Honoring God never is. So before you sign it, be sure you mean it. Search your heart and determine if you are ready to follow Christ's heart and to give up pleasing yourself. Frankly, I believe it is your only choice if you want to call yourself a follower of the Messiah. Are you ready?

Mind Control

Dear Hayley,

Help! I don't know why, but at church I am really nice, and as soon as I get to school, I change into a meany. I hang out with girls who pick on people and talk about them. I don't know how else to fit in, so I do the same thing. How can I be the same person at school and church?

Meany

Dear Meany,

You make a choice to be who you are. You've made the choice to follow the crowd and be mean. If you want to change, all you have to do is make the choice. Once you've done that, try this:

1. Write down all the verses from the Bible on loving others, including on loving your enemies.
2. Write a letter to God telling him how you want to change. Tell him what you've done wrong and what you want to do from now on. Read it every morning before you go to school. This will help you to renew your mind to be the Girl Grown Up he wants you to be.
3. When you are with your clique and they start dissing people, tell them you have a problem with gossip, so you have to leave because you don't want to love it so much. Then walk away. They'll learn from your actions that what they are doing is wrong, and if they are convicted, they will stop too.
4. Practice complimenting people and being nice. Be nice to 3 people every day—people you wouldn't ordinarily be nice to. Do it!

I know it's hard. That's tough. You wanna make a choice to be a godly girl, you're gonna have to do some work. You can do it. I know you can.

"It is doubtful that God can use anyone greatly until He has hurt him deeply."

—A. W. Tozer

Mean = Murder

In the movie *Minority Report* starring Tom Cruise, the government of the future has developed the technology to read people's thoughts from a central location in the city. They use this technology to arrest future criminals before they ever even commit a crime. In this surrealistic play on a spiritual theme, they are able to judge people guilty of evil thoughts and to punish them before they do anything to anyone.

As I watched the film, I realized how much we take our ability to think private thoughts for granted, certain that no one would ever eavesdrop. How much would my thoughts change if I were judged for them as soon as I had them? What if what I thought and plotted and planned actually had a consequence in some realm? The movie really got me to thinking.

Some 2000 years before the movie, on the side of a mountain in Galilee, Jesus sat down with a bunch of his followers and began to explain a similar idea to them. Can you imagine the scene? (Read it in the book of Matthew, chapter 5, verses 27–28.) As they watched him and hung on every word, he looked at them and said, "You have heard that it was said, 'Do not commit adultery.'" Everyone in the crowd probably nodded and looked at each other in agreement. Jesus went on, "But I tell you that anyone who looks at a woman lustfully has already committed adultery with her in his heart." This probably shocked the audience. For them, *thinking* had never been mentioned alongside of *doing* before.

Could he have meant it? Really? Is it really a sin to just think of sex with someone other than your spouse? Why not? If the police of *Minority Report* could see people's thoughts, how much more can God? You know that he is omniscient (all-knowing) and therefore knows everything you think before you even say it, right?

"Crime doesn't consist in the deed but in the will."

—Rufinus

"Before a word is on my tongue you know it completely, O LORD" (Psalm number 139, verse 4). So why wouldn't God convict you of your thoughts? To him they are no different than your actions. That's what Jesus told his disciples.

Are you sitting down for this one? He has more to say about your thoughts than just this stuff about sex. Did you know God says that when you have angry or mean thoughts about someone, you get the same punishment as a murderer?

> You have heard that it was said to those of old, "You shall not murder; and whoever murders will be liable to judgment." But I say to you that everyone who is angry with his brother will be liable to judgment; whoever insults his brother will be liable to the council; and whoever says, "You fool!" will be liable to the hell of fire.
>
> Matthew 5:21–22 ESV

So think about it like this: Your thoughts are no longer secret. If you think you can let your mind wander or fantasize about what you are going to do to a certain girl, think again. You aren't alone in your head, even if it feels like you are. God's tuned in to all your thoughts—the good, the bad, and the ugly. How does that make you feel? Invaded? Scared? Loved? Think about it. He's involved in all your thinking. Are you happy about that right now? If not, then what do you want to do to change? Because he isn't going anywhere. He'll always be listening. Always taking note and responding to your thoughts.

I worked at a restaurant in Portland, Oregon. I was a server. It was a really busy place, and we worked our butts off. The thing that really shocked

> It is dangerous for the mind to dwell on what is forbidden, to perform, and to plan out sin rashly. Even without carrying out our sinful desires, what we will is considered done. Therefore, it will be punished as an action. . . . Don't will it if you won't carry it out. By your mind's confession you condemn yourself.
>
> —Tertullian

me, since it was my first restaurant experience, was how cranky all the servers were about their customers. Sure, they're nice to your face, but you'd never believe what they say behind your back. "That woman is driving me crazy!" one would scream. "I've never seen such an idiot in all my life," another would say. And the conversations went on like that all night. "I hate this guy." "I want to kill this woman." "Who does he think he is?" They rattled on and on. As I stood at the counter by the moaning staff, I did one of those daze things, like a dream sequence, where all the words just start to fade into each other and you think, *What is all this chatter?* And then suddenly it hit me: This must be what the world sounds like to God. All our complaining and moaning. All our evil thoughts and angry fantasies. He has to listen to everyone's bad days and cranky moments. How ungrateful we must sound to his giving ears. How miserable we are as we bring him into our pity parties and hissy fits. It's ugly, really, when you think about it. Noise pollution in the spiritual realm.

How much do you contribute to the noise pollution that God endures? What kind of stuff do you throw up to your Savior daily? Are your thoughts kind, grateful, and loving, or are they angry, hateful, and bitter? Which do you think pleases him most?

> "Try to find out what is pleasing to the Lord."
> —Paul's letter to the Ephesians, chapter 5, verse 10 NLT

One of my favorite verses is from Philippians 4:8. It's all about your thoughts—what they should be focused on. Paul tells the Philippians that they should think about good stuff, not bad stuff. Honorable, excellent, stuff like that. Now, as I see it, this is a good idea for two major reasons. One is that you are what you think. If you think nasty thoughts, you are a nasty person. If you think depressing thoughts, you are a depressing person. So you end up getting whatever you think most about. But the second reason is that God has to listen to your thoughts. And he takes them seriously. So if you want to honor him and please him, thinking good stuff is one major step on the way to doing that. So how about you?

> Are you proud of your thoughts?
>
> What do you think about most of the time?
>
> What do you think when you think about your enemies?
>
> Do you think more happy thoughts or angry thoughts?
>
> If you could be convicted for your thoughts, what would you be convicted of?

In one way or another, my girls, you are the sum total of your thoughts. What you think about most tells you what you value, who you are, what you want, what you love, and all kinds of things. If I were to look at your thoughts, who would I see? Would you be proud? Answer these questions seriously and take some time to think about what you think about most.

Environmental Quiz

Take this quiz to find out what your spiritual pollution level is. Don't lie to yourself—God is listening.

1. When I lie in bed, I usually think about:
   a. the bad parts of my day
   b. how to get back at people
   c. all the stuff I'm thankful for
2. When my mind wanders, it's usually stuck on:
   a. thinking of ways to get revenge
   b. worrying about stuff people did to me
   c. the amazing God that I serve
3. Most of the time I feel:
   a. depressed
   b. bored
   c. happy
4. My parents say that I'm:
   a. a whiner
   b. depressed
   c. well balanced
5. When I'm with my friends, we mainly talk about:
   a. how much we hate other girls
   b. how miserable our lives are
   c. how cool our lives are
6. At my school/work:
   a. there is at least one girl who hates me
   b. there are several girls that I can't stand
   c. there are all kinds of people, but I like them all
7. If God is listening in on my thoughts, he is:
   a. not happy with me
   b. not listening anymore 'cuz he's sick of me
   c. proud of me

8. I want to change my thoughts and make them better.
     True   False

Add up your points:

1. a = 1, b = 1, c = 3
2. a = 1, b = 2, c = 3
3. a = 1, b = 2, c = 3
4. a = 1, b = 1, c = 3
5. a = 1, b = 1, c = 3
6. a = 2, b = 1, c = 3
7. a = 1, b = 1, c = 3
8. T = 3, F = 1

8–18: Polluter! Take it easy on the negative thoughts! You don't have to be so down on everything. Remember, you are what you think, so you must be pretty miserable. If you want to feel better, try changing your negative way of thinking to a more positive one. It will be a hard change, but you can do it. I believe in you. Read over the next chapter, *Saving the Spiritual Environment,* and see if you can't change the spiritual environment you are creating.

19–24: Environmentally sound. Congrats! Looks like you are taking care of your spiritual environment, keeping things clean and healthy. Keep up the good work. God is proud of you and so am I.

Saving the Spiritual Environment

If you are a polluter, someone who treats your thoughts like a giant waste dump, but now you want to change, what do you do? How do you stop the spiritual pollution? The first step is to want to. That's the major hurdle for most people. They don't want to stop thinking bad thoughts, because they like them too much. So deciding to stop is the first step. It's a step that Scripture talks about all the time. It's called repentance.

How's it done? It's easy. It's all about telling God what you did, how you hate it, and how you want to change. (Check this out in 1 John 1:9 and Proverbs 28:13.) God knows what you think, so you aren't doing this for his good but for your own. You have to break yourself down enough to admit you were wrong. That's a biggie. You know how hard it can be to say, "I was wrong." Confession is just that—saying you were wrong. And it's a crucial part of changing your ways (repentance). So tell God the jerk you've been, and then tell him thank you for forgiving you for it. Because remember, no matter what you have done, if you are a Christian you are already forgiven as soon as you confess (see 1 John 1:9). It's the reason Jesus died, and it's crucial to understand (see Hebrews 12:2). So your job is to confess your junk and then thank him for the forgiveness his Word says you have.

> "If we confess our sins, he is faithful and just and will forgive us our sins and purify us from all unrighteousness."
>
> 1 John 1:9

After you've gone through the confession, then you can get on to the renewing (Romans 12:2). You've created a nasty habit of thinking bad thoughts. And habits take time to change. Just because you confess and are forgiven doesn't mean it all magically disappears and bam!, you're a new woman. Change is hard, and it takes effort. So here's the 411. You've gotta play mind police. Lay down the law, believe the law, and enforce the law. The law is just your list of things you are going to do or not do. You know your thoughts better than I do, so you can make your own law. Just base it on Philippians 4:8. What won't you think anymore? What will you think about?

Next, enforcing the law. This is harder than it sounds, if that's possible. Now that you've agreed with God on what you will and won't let yourself think, it's time to keep yourself honest. The best way to do this is to stop yourself every time you start to think the wrong things. And the best way to do that is to say "no" out loud (or quietly under your breath, if other people are around). Just say "no." Your thoughts will be like, "What? You're telling me no? What's the meaning of this?" But don't worry. They'll get the hang of it. Now, once you've stopped the bad thought, you have to replace it with a good thought or it'll just come right back (see Matthew 12:44–45). The way to do that is to think something good, something holy. Pray for the person. Think of it as adoring Christ. Thank God for something he has done for you—you shouldn't have to look too far to find something. Whatever you do, replace that ungodly thought with a godly one.

> Finally, brothers,
> whatever is true,
> whatever is noble,
> whatever is right,
> whatever is pure,
> whatever is lovely,
> whatever is admirable
> —if anything is
> excellent
> or praiseworthy
> —think about
> such things.
>
> Philippians 4:8

Remember, just thinking a bad thought doesn't mean you're bad; it just means you're tempted. If it did mean you were bad, then we would have to think Jesus was bad, and we know he wasn't. "For we do not have a high priest who is unable to sympathize with our weaknesses, but we have one who has been tempted in every way, just as we are—yet was without sin" (Hebrews 4:15).

Satan tempted Jesus with evil thoughts, but Jesus shut him down by saying no to

> **"Do not conform any longer to the pattern of this world, but be transformed by the renewing of your mind. Then you will be able to test and approve what God's will is—his good, pleasing and perfect will."**
> **Romans 12:2**

them and replacing those thoughts with the truth (read how he did it in Matthew chapter 4). Scripture is your best weapon for fighting bad thoughts. So your job right now is to collect your weapons, just like Jesus did. Write down 5 verses that are truth you can hold on to when you start to think bad stuff. Things like Romans 8:28 are good. Get all 5 verses onto cards or a sheet of paper you can carry around with you. You're gonna need 'em.

If you want to have a healthy and clean spirit and a loving relationship with your God, practice creating a clean spiritual environment by controlling your thoughts.*

"Good thoughts and actions
can never produce bad results;
bad thoughts and actions
can never produce good results.
This is but saying that
nothing can come from corn
but corn,
nothing from nettles
but nettles."
—James Allen

*For more help on this topic, pick up the book *As a Man Thinketh* by James Allen.

Is Your Friend a Mean Girl?

Mean Girls aren't always your enemies—sometimes they are your friends. Ask yourself these Qs to find out if your friends are mean:

Do you feel worse after hanging out with your friend?   **Yes   No**

Do you have to be careful about what you say?   **Yes   No**

Is she the last person you call when your world falls apart?   **Yes   No**

Does she get jealous when your life goes well?   **Yes   No**

Does she get mad when you tell her no?   **Yes   No**

Does she make you feel guilty when you won't do what she wants to do?   **Yes   No**

If you answered yes to most of these, your friend might be a Mean Girl.

A Mean Girl
can be fun to be with
and be hurting you
at the same time.

10 Clues Your Friend Is Bad News

She's your best friend. You do everything together, but you just don't think you like her anymore. Maybe she's changed lately, or maybe you've changed. Either way, she's driving you crazy, and you don't know what to do but you don't want the grief anymore. It sucks, I know. Let me be the first to tell you that it is okay to break up with your friends. In fact, you have the choice to stop being friends with anyone you don't want to be friends with anymore.

As believers we are always told to love people, and we should. But loving people doesn't always mean being friends with them. Sometimes being friends with them is actually harming both them and you. So step back and figure it out. If you've read some stuff in this book that makes you think your friend is a Mean Girl, then it might be time for a friend change.

Double-check this list to see if she fits any of these. If she does, ask yourself if you are being faithful by allowing her to be mean.

■ 10 Clues Your Friend Is Bad News

1. **She's overly defensive.** You can never tell her if she does something wrong, because she just flips out.

2. **She loves to talk about other people.** If she spends most of her time talking about other people, then beware, because she's probably talking about you when you aren't around.

3. **She loves revenge.** Don't ever cross her because she'll get even. She doesn't let anybody get her. She's revenge central.

4. **She's religious, not spiritual.** She lives by a strict list of right and wrong, and if you don't agree with her, she

judges you. Sometimes she acts so holier-than-thou that you are just sure she's faking it. Don't hang out with a fraud, or your faith will begin to suffer.

5. *She's always gotta look good.* If she's scared to look stupid, then she's probably really cranky when she does something stupid. Mean girls don't want to be laughed at, and if they are, their anger flares.

6. *It's all about her.* If she doesn't care about how other people feel, then she's not a safe friend.

7. *She always flatters you.* Flattery feels great, but when it's all someone does, you might start to wonder what they want from you. Friends are people who can be honest with you and don't always have to stroke your ego to make you like them.

8. *She never forgives.* Forgiveness is a command from God. Don't forgive and you won't be forgiven, and a soul that can't forgive is a soul that isn't faithful to God's Word. If she never forgives and never forgets, then she might be making your life miserable.

9. *She's jealous of your wins.* If she can't celebrate with you when things go great for you, she might just be jealous. Jealousy is a dangerous beast and can flare up in many different ways. If she tends to prefer it when you are miserable, she isn't a true friend.

10. *You feel worse after talking or being with her.* Friends should make us feel better, not worse. If you feel bad after being with her, something is wrong. Whether it's something she does or something she says, you shouldn't consistently feel worse after talking to a friend.

How to Handle Your Mean Friends

Mean Girls aren't always so easy to spot—sometimes they aren't even your enemies; they are your friends. And you don't even really think of them as mean. You might think of them as a pain sometimes, but are they really mean? Well, the main question you have to ask is, Are they helping you to be the girl you want to be? Or are they making you feel icky, tired, wounded, and depressed? You might think it's just your problem, but those friends who bring you down might actually be toxic to your system. They might be a path to destruction and a distraction from who you are. But can you find a way around it? Can you help your friend out of her toxic dump? Or do you just need to dump her? Let's have a look.

The Complainer

You know her—all she wants to do is whine to you about her miserable life. "So and so did this, my mom did that, my life stinks, blah, blah, blah." And any time you try to show her the good side, she just freaks out and says you don't understand her, her pain isn't that easy to just get over, she's sick of looking at the good side, and on and on the story goes.

THE COMPLAINER AND YOU

If you're like most of us, you give in to this girl. You realize that if you are all happy and hopeful, she thinks you are a waste of her time. She needs sympathy, so you get dragged down into her misery in order to sympathize. Sound healthy? No, because it's not. Another person's bad mood or outlook shouldn't mean you have to have the same outlook in order to be their friend. With this kind of friend, you can end up with serious problems, from depression to low self-esteem. Heck, your homework might even suffer if she is unrelenting in her moping and brings you with her! A true friend wants the best for you, not the worst.

A friend wants you to be happy and healthy, not dark and depressed. So don't give in to her whining. Don't join in; don't agree. Don't feed her negativity.

How to Deal with the Complainer

1. Ask her what's wrong.
2. If she really has major problems, ask her to talk to a counselor or pastor.
3. If her problems aren't life-threatening but just a continual drip in her emotional-turmoil-tank, then maybe it's time to fess up. Let her know that you aren't up for all the drama. If her darkness is making your life roll off track, then she might not be a good friend for you. She might just be a Mean Girl in disguise, and if that's the case and she's a believer, God calls you to "admonish" her. *"Let the word of Christ dwell in you richly, teaching and admonishing one another in all wisdom"* (Colossians 3:16 ESV). Huh? Wondering what the heck that means? According to Webster's, *admonish* means:

> **1 a:** to indicate duties or obligations to
> **b:** to express warning or disapproval to, especially in a gentle, earnest, or solicitous manner
> **2:** to give friendly earnest advice or encouragement to

What that all means is that as believers we are called to remind each other about God's law and to do it in a friendly way. So you can remind the complainer of verses like *"Do everything without complaining or arguing"* (Philippians 2:14). Or check out the verse list at the end of this book for a verse that suits her complaining woes. I know this part can be totally hard, but hard faith builds good faith muscles. If you are devoted to pleasing God, then admonishing your sister is your only option.

4. If she is a non-believer, you have to act from another angle. She won't be easily changed by your correcting her with Scripture, since it means nothing to her, but her pain does have an answer in Scripture. The Scripture she needs isn't words that admonish her but words that save her. Her pain is a perfect opportunity to tell her about the saving grace of Jesus. After all, he is the answer to each of her aches and pains. Don't let her drag you down into her faithless life, but use the power of Christ within you to lift her up. Check out the Gospel on page 179 and *Choosing Christ* on page 204 or go to <u>www.meangirls.net</u> for more ideas on how to share your faith.

5. Remember, not saying or doing anything won't change a thing. If you are tired of Miss Mopey, then get to changing your own life. She might never change, but you have the power to change your life and the responsibility to give her hope for hers.

The Gossip Hound

This kind of friend seems totally fun to have around. She has all the hot G, and she loves to share it. Your bond gets deeper and deeper with each nasty little secret. But do you trust her? I mean, if you have a major trauma, do you go to her with it? Or do you know by now that there's no way she can be trusted? After all, she lives for good G. Does that include yours? A gossipy friend can spell disaster for you. First of all it means that nothing you say is safe. No matter what, if you tell her something, you can be sure everyone else will hear about it. And soon you find yourself censoring everything before you say it. The result is stress. When you can't relax with your friend, you aren't really with a friend. The second big deal about having a gossipy friend is that she feeds your tendency to want the juice. She leads you into places you know you really don't want to go. She feeds your appetite for other people's destruction. Gossip is a destroyer of people. The book of Proverbs says it, *"As surely as a wind from the north brings rain, so a gossiping tongue causes anger!"* (25:23 NLT).

THE GOSSIP HOUND AND YOU

With this girl you find yourself in one of two positions: either you clam up because you are afraid that she will blab all your stuff, or you dive into her flow and start craving more good stuff. Either way, is this a safe relationship or a toxic one? You have to ask yourself if your friend is a Mean Girl or a good friend. Are you supporting the enemy or the good guys? Whoever you are hanging out with, you are telling the rest of the world that you support that person and believe in them and who they are. You are saying that the kind of person they are is okay with you. So think about it: Is that true?

HOW TO DEAL WITH THE GOSSIP HOUND

1. First of all, don't think of your friend as a lost cause. If she has no understanding of the meanness of gossip, then she has no reason to stop. So start to talk to her about it. Tell her what you think. Ask her what she thinks. Don't judge and condemn her; just talk about it openly. You gotta start talking it out, because that's the only real way to help others. You've gotta help her see that what she is doing is hurting other people.

2. "As iron sharpens iron, so one man sharpens another" (Proverbs 27:17). What do you think it feels like to be sharpened? Imagine having a sharp piece of metal rubbing against you, rubbing down the edges and sharpening up the corners. It's painful. And talking to your gossiping friend won't be painless either, for you or for her. But if you are called to be an honest friend, you have to start chatting and figuring out how you both can be more faithful to the truth that gossip is bad news.

3. Whatever you do, don't think that you have to gossip to keep her as a friend. What's more important, your spirit or keeping her happy? Choose today who you want to be and then stick to it. If you want to be more like Christ, then give up on the gossip. It might make her mad, but who would you rather tick off—your friend or God?

The Dictator

This friend has convinced herself *and you* that she is the better one. She is smarter, holier, more fun, the list goes on and on. She really likes you, but she wants you to understand that she knows what's best for both of you and she won't take no for an answer. She can choose better things to do, better people to be with, and better thoughts to think. And hey, sometimes you think *Why not go along? It's better than making her mad.* Because if you don't do what she wants, she's gonna let you know about it. And you don't need all that turmoil. If you aren't sure whether your friend is a dictator, practice saying no to her and see how she reacts. If she freaks out and won't let you be you, then beware, you might be a pawn in her kingdom.

"The need to control and peace of mind can't occur at the same time."
—Lee Jampolsky

THE DICTATOR AND YOU

The dictator makes you feel kinda stupid. Whenever you talk to her, you feel dumb, like you just don't get things. Her mission, however covert it is, is to make you inferior. Why? Because that makes her superior. She's probably treating you more like her minion than her friend, always deciding things for you and never taking your no for an answer. It just isn't an option to disagree with her. You might even start to feel dependent on her, like you really need her. After all, she *is* the better one. Check yourself if you have a friend who makes you feel like this. Friends should build you up. They aren't always right, they aren't always the smartest, and they shouldn't be afraid to tell you. A true friend will admit to being wrong. She will let you see her weaknesses and share her fears with you. She won't act like she has everything together all the time.

How to Deal with the Dictator

You have a responsibility in this relationship. When you let her bully her way through life, you keep her from growing spiritually. Part of growing is being broken and being wrong. It's the whole iron sharpening iron thing—it hurts but it's necessary. "As iron sharpens iron, a friend sharpens a friend" (Proverbs 27:17 NLT).

1. Check out these verses about friendship and see if you are a true friend to this Mean Girl: James 5:16; Ecclesiastes 4:10.
2. Don't be afraid to be honest with her. The dictator needs someone to tell her no and to tell her the truth about her mean behavior. "Wounds from a friend can be trusted, but an enemy multiplies kisses" (Proverbs 27:6). This verse doesn't mean that you should let your friend keep on hurting you or that you should start hurting her. What it means is that friends are *real* with each other. They help each other grow and learn, and part of growing hurts. That's why they are called "growing pains." Confronting your fears or your friend can be freaky,

> "A close relationship hurts, because no perfect people live on earth."
> —Dr. Henry Cloud and Dr. John Townsend, *Safe People*

She says she's sorry so you won't be mad at her, not because she sincerely is sorry and wants to change.

but friends who allow you to do that can be trusted.

3. Tell her no. Like I said earlier, you have to be able to say no to her if she is a real friend. Friendships will wither up and die if you aren't allowed to disagree. Disagreeing is a normal part of life, and if you spend all your energy trying to make her happy rather than just sticking to what you believe, you are building an unhealthy relationship. Galatians 1:10 says, "Am I now trying to win the approval of men, or of God? Or am I trying to please men? If I were still trying to please men, I would not be a servant of Christ."

▌ The Sorry Sister

The Sorry Sister is always apologizing for the stuff she's done. Trouble is, it never seems to change anything. "Sorry" doesn't cut it if it isn't coupled with a change, and this sister just won't change. She says she's sorry so you won't be mad at her, not because she sincerely is sorry and wants to change. A lot of the time she's just sorry that you're mad or hurt, not sorry about what she did. But she doesn't necessarily even know that. She's too obsessed with making sure everybody likes her.

THE SORRY SISTER AND YOU

This kind of friend can almost make you feel crazy. You want to accept her apol-

"Never ask the advice of another about anything God makes you decide before Him. If you ask advice, you will nearly always side with Satan: 'Immediately I conferred not with flesh and blood.'"
—Oswald Chambers, *My Utmost for His Highest*

ogy—after all, it is an apology—but deep down you know it doesn't mean anything. But you think maybe it's just you. Maybe you are overreacting. But maybe not. If she is always sorry and never changing, then the problem is hers, not yours. Don't let someone else's character flaw become your nightmare.

How to Deal with the Sorry Sister

1. Maybe she doesn't realize what she's doing. As a friend, it's part of your job to point out areas in her life that are keeping her from being a good person. (Don't go overboard on this and become a Mean Girl yourself, always pointing out someone's faults. But in moderation, as appropriate, we all need input on our character flaws.) So let her know that she's saying she's sorry but she's not changing. Let her know that sorry doesn't cut it because it's not about what you say but what you do, and words are meaningless if not accompanied by a change in action (read it in 2 Corinthians 7:10; Acts 26:20).

2. If she still keeps it up once you've let her know how you feel, you should consider a change of friends. You can't keep letting her lie to herself and you. It's not faithful of you to let people continue to live a lie. (See *Standing Up to Believers*, page 110.)

Don't let someone else's character flaw become your nightmare.

The Perfect Girl

The Perfect Girl is too perfect to be wrong. She's too with it, in her mind, to be wrong. Ever! I mean, it's always someone *else's* fault. And she doesn't forgive them, either. Her mom ruined her life. Her teacher hates her. Someone's always after her, and it's never for a good reason, because she is, after all, perfect. When she *does* get caught doing something wrong, she will never admit it. She can't handle confrontation, either. She doesn't want to hear what other people think, because life's all about *her*. She never takes responsibility for anything in her life.

THE PERFECT GIRL AND YOU

With the Perfect Girl you feel like you are always fighting a battle. It becomes exhausting listening to the list of people in her life who are after her. She wants your sympathy, and she wants you to fight the injustice with her, because she's never wrong. It can often become a gripe session about how awful "everybody else" is.

HOW TO DEAL WITH THE PERFECT GIRL

1. Don't let her get away with lying to herself or to you. This girl is a tough one. But if you never admit you are wrong, then you can never grow, and that's what's happened to her. You probably already know that if you attempt to correct her and intercept a lie she is telling herself, she will probably get angry with you, but you can't continue to feed her fantasy. "He who listens to a life-giving rebuke will be at home among the wise" (Proverbs 15:31).

2. Think about moving on. The Perfect Girl is so defensive that when you confront her, she tends to give you all her pain. She won't take any of it on herself. "He who ignores discipline despises himself, but whoever heeds correction gains understanding" (Proverbs 15:32). So if that's the case, it might be time to move on. Be true to who you were meant to be—a faithful friend, but not one who gives in to someone just to keep the peace.

> True friends will tell you the truth even at the risk of you leaving them. They will risk making you mad in order to love you.

■ The Really Mean Girl

The Really Mean Girl is easy to spot. We've been talking about her all over this book. Her goal is to torture other people. And she tortures them well. If the Really Mean Girl is your friend, you might feel safe—at least while she likes you, you aren't going to be under her attack. But are you really safe? Think about it like this: Does she use you? Does she make you do things you really aren't up for? Does she do things that make you feel uncomfortable? If so, then you might be guilty by association with a Really Mean Girl friend. That is, you have become a Mean Girl accomplice, and the world sees you as mean.

THE REALLY MEAN GIRL AND YOU

The Really Mean Girl is probably in control of your life. You feel like you have to follow her lead or she'll get mad at you. You really like her when she's nice, but look out when she's mad. You probably like how important she makes you feel when she tells you all her latest plans or the big gossip around town. But deep down you know what she's doing is wrong. You know that it hurts other girls, but you are too afraid to get her to stop. With this Mean Girl, you are a pawn. You are being used by her to further her agenda, and yes, if she did lose interest in you or get mad at you, your friendship could end instantly. In fact, I have news for you: This isn't a friendship at all. This is a tyranny. She is controlling you for her own agenda. And that isn't friendship; it's manipulation (Proverbs 17:17; 22:24). When you are with your Mean Girl, you might feel safe, but this is a false safety because you are not only building a friendship with someone who is dangerous, you are also piling spiritual destruction on yourself. The things you do because of her will not go unpunished.

God has called us to be holy, not to live impure lives. Anyone who refuses to live by these rules is not disobeying human rules but is rejecting God, who gives his Holy Spirit to you.

1 Thessalonians 4:7–8 NLT

Pleading ignorance or being under someone else's control will not set you free. You can't follow Christ and the Really Mean Girl at the same time. As Christ himself says in Luke 16:13, "No one can serve two masters. For you will hate one and love the other, or be devoted to one and despise the other." She will be your destruction if you don't get away from her meanness.

HOW TO DEAL WITH THE REALLY MEAN GIRL

1. **Get honest.** The first thing you have to do is to be honest with yourself. Admit that she has a problem and that her problem has become yours. You are not immune to her meanness; you are her partner in crime if you are her friend. First admit your guilt, and then you can begin to do something about it.

2. **Pray for forgiveness.** You can do it right now.

   Dear Father God, I confess that I have let _____ run my life and make me a Mean Girl too. I no longer want to be her pawn in the life of mean, and I want to be free from her control. I believe that I was wrong in trying to please her over you. That is idolatry, and I know you will not stand for it. Please forgive me for my ignorance and for lying to myself. I want to be honest from now on and commit to living by your Word rather than hers. Thank you for letting me start fresh. Today is a new day, and I will make the best of it, forgetting what is behind and pushing forward to win the prize you have set for me. Amen.

Check out *Standing Up to the Believer* (page 110) and *Standing Up to the Non-Believer* (page 109) for more help on this.

3. Pray for her.

Father, _____ is a Mean Girl. She seems to be out of control. I know I don't have the power to change her, but you do. Please open her eyes to your truth and help her to learn to love. Show me how to be a guide to her and what to say to her when I talk to her next. Help me to know your Word so that I know what to say the next time she starts to be mean. Give me the strength to resist her meanness and to help her with the truth. Amen.

4. Read *Changing a Mean Girl* (page 93) and *God's Plan for Your Mean Girl* (page 115).

5. Talk to her.
When you do, remember, it isn't about condemning her or judging her. That won't get you anywhere. What you want to do is tell her about yourself and what you want for your life. Let her know you've been convicted by reading this book and that you want to change your life to please God. Tell her what you won't be doing anymore. Make a list beforehand so you don't get off track when she argues with you. This isn't about her just yet—it's about you. So stay on track. She will probably instantly feel judged and convicted no matter what you say, but that isn't because of you; it's because her own spirit is convicting her. Let her feel what she will feel. Your job isn't to make her feel better right now. When you've said your piece, give her time to process it. How you handle your Mean Girl friend will depend on her position with Christ.

6. Look it up.
If you feel strong enough to still be her friend, beware. You will find it hard not to fall back into her mean ways. You will still be associated with her because of all the times you've been on her side of the attack. So **think**

about these verses before you decide what to do next: Amos 3:3; 1 Corinthians 5:11; Proverbs 20:19; Proverbs 22:24. And remember, in the words of the apostle Paul, "bad company corrupts good character" (1 Corinthians 15:33).

7. **Repent.** If you finally admit that you too were a Mean Girl, then it's time to become a Girl Grown Up (see page 134) and do the right thing. God calls us to confess our sins—that is, to ask forgiveness from the person you hurt. This is going to totally suck. And don't expect the girl you hurt to immediately forgive you. She probably doesn't trust you because of your history with your Really Mean Girl friend, but you still have to do it. If you're ready to start putting God above yourself, do this right away and without fear.

8. **Talk to God.** Now that you have read a large amount of this book and heard what God's Word has to say about friends, you know what to talk to him about. Spend some time alone with him. Go somewhere you won't be disturbed. Bring a Bible, maybe play some worship music, and get alone with him. Confess and listen. Hear what he has to tell you about your next steps and your future. If you hear something in your head that is inconsistent with Scripture, then question whose voice it is. God will never contradict Scripture. So go to the back of this book (page 190) and get some good verses in your head. Then just listen to God as he fills you with his truth.

I know that this change in your friend pattern will be totally hard, but it's time to take your life back from your mean friends. Trust God—his Word is useful for all your needs and will never leave you ashamed.

Bad company

corrupts

good character.

—the apostle Paul

Girls as Friends: Why Is It Easier to Be Friends with Guys?

If you just don't get girls and never have, or if you think guys are easier to get along with but you know you need girlfriends, or if you are just ready to make some true friends instead of mean friends, listen up!

I know how hard it is to be friends with girls. Believe me, it takes a lot of work. Guys are so much easier to hang out with. They aren't so emotional. They don't get so freaked out on ya, and they are just plain fun to be with. But that's no excuse to avoid girls altogether. And you might not believe me right now, but someday you're gonna need girls. God made us for communion with other girls. He didn't make it so that all our lives we would be surrounded by guys only. Certain things we can only get from other girls, and certain things we should only *give* to other girls. Take it from this girl. Katie knows what it's like to need girls. She's a 9-year-old aspiring writer friend of mine and has yet to decide that girls are the enemy. Remember the day?

Being a girl is great! Especially because we girls have about three times the imagination of boys. I wonder why boys sit and play Gamecube and watch TV while we girls pamper ourselves with the most, uh, creative things. (Oops! Just a thought.)

I have nothing at all wrong with guy friends. It's just at the moment I like especially stickin' with the girls.

Girls will always understand you, but boys, uh, no. Boys don't even seem human. If you have feelings, you can tell a boy, but they won't understand. They will just blink and then repeat something that seems like the exact opposite thing. If you have a boy that's your best friend, your life is simple and plain. No insult to the males, but you are stuck with a diary to talk to, and even though you can tell your diary all the things that happen to you, a diary isn't there to, well, suffer the pain with you, and understand you. Trust me, you need comfort from your own gender.

Boys don't exactly understand us girls—you know, your feelings—like girls do. Having girl friends can help your life. Girls are by far the best.

Katie P., age 9

Katie gets it. Girls are important. And as you get older, what you are doing by surrounding yourself with girls (and by that I mean you have at least 3 good girlfriends) is preparing for your future. I know the future seems like a long way off, but it isn't, believe me. And if you can learn now how to be friends with girls, you will save yourself a lot of heartache in the future. Guys will come and go, but if you keep your friendships strong, you will always have a shoulder to cry on. And when you finally find "the one," your girlfriends will relieve a lot of the stress that you could put on him by being there to pick up the girl slack. See, guys don't need to know everything about us. When they do, they just get overwhelmed. It's too much to hear that your cramps really hurt today and that you feel ugly because you don't have any new clothes. It's a bore to hear that you hate your hair or that your cat did the cutest thing today. Most guys can't handle all that we want to say, and that's why we need girls. So give the guy in your life a break and get some girlfriends.

But how do you be friends with girls? If you are anything like I was, you don't have a clue how to make friends with girls. So here are a few pointers to help you out. Remember, it's essential to have girlfriends, but more than 3 is overkill, because you won't have time to be good friends to that many girls, so none of them will be getting enough of your attention. So here are the things you need to know about finding girlfriends:

1. *Effort*—It's all about the effort. You have to be looking for them. You can't expect them to come to you and to do all the work. That's right, work! Making friends requires work, especially when it comes to girls. It might require that you call them a couple times a week just to talk, or in some cases just to listen. (Girls love to talk!) It might require that you ask them to do things with you. Don't wait for them to ask, even if you are shy. I realized a couple of years ago that I never asked girls to do anything because I was afraid of rejection. I had been rejected by girls for so long that I feared rejection even in adulthood, so I never approached any of them to do anything with me. When I realized what I was doing, I decided to get over it and get on with life, and I started asking them to lunch, to the movies, to dinner, and all kinds of things. Some of them said no, they were too busy, and I had to fight the fear of rejection, but I fought it and went on. Finally I found some who were really excited to be with me, and their answer was more often yes. I am so thankful that I gave it a shot and took the risk. I don't know where I'd be today without my dear friends.

2. *Maintain the love*—Girls usually need more attention than guys. I know that I could go an entire month without calling my guy friends, but once we talked again it was like we had been together all month. They didn't hold a grudge against me for not calling. But girls are just different. They kinda like to be kept in the loop. So here are some ideas to help them feel loved:

- *send an e-card for no reason*
- *drop them a note in the mail*
- *call just to see how their day is going*
- *put a note in their locker saying "Hi"*

- *buy them a gift, like their favorite candy or magazine*
- *pick a flower and give it to them*
- *find a way to let them know you are thinking about them. Get creative. It doesn't take too much time or energy.*

3. Learn to speak girlese—If you aren't used to being around girls, then a few pointers on how they communicate might help you out. Let's start with how guys talk for comparison. Guys usually communicate like a football game. The guy *telling* the story is on offense; the *listener* is on defense. At some point the guy on offense scores and kicks the ball off to the other team (guy), who then takes the ball and is off onto *his* story. Passing off and whose ball it is are clear. They always have a goal in mind—a point that one guy must get to so that the other guy can then take the ball. Getting to the point is crucial in guy world.

Girls, on the other hand, usually communicate like a game of Twister. We pick a subject and get to talking on it. Another girl interrupts with a comment on the topic, and then it goes back to the first girl. Interruptions occur frequently and may take the story off topic for a few minutes, but we get back on topic with a kind, "I'm sorry, I just had to say that. Now where were you?" The goal for girls often isn't anything more than just speaking—most of the time, we don't have to have a point. We don't have to find a fix for our problems or work anything out by the end of the conversation. We feel better if we can just tell another person about it. This freaks guys out! Guys want to get to an end, to have a point. That's why girl talk can be frustrating to guys. We don't need to figure anything out; we just need to dump and then we are all better. Guys don't dump, generally. They work things out alone in their head and save talking for something with a point. Their whole goal in a conversation is to get to the point, not to just talk with no end in sight.

If you are used to guy talk, hanging out with girls might be a little challenging to you. It was for me. Gab, gab, gab. But remember, with girls you can interrupt, change the subject, and make comments. It's girlese. Watch how they talk and start to notice their need to just blab. If you listen, you score, but if you blab some yourself, you score big too. Being able to just dump your emotions on someone who gets you is the most amazing feeling. And girls get that part of you better than any guy ever could.

The Big Picture: Helping Your School Become Unmean

Let me just take this chance to say congratulations. Congrats on making it this far and on the changes you've put yourself through. It's hard work, this sanctification stuff, setting yourself apart for obedience to God's Word. But in the end the payoff is supreme. God doesn't want you to stop with yourself, though. No, he wants you to spread the love. All over the Bible we are called to make disciples and lead others to repentance. I bet you never really knew how you fit into that whole scene. Well, now you do. It's as simple as helping other girls learn what you've learned and helping your school or where you work to become a Mean-Free Zone.

Imagine if your school were free of Mean Girls. Imagine if no girl ever had to feel the sting of rejection or hatred. Imagine a place where God's Word reigned supreme. I know, that seems like a stretch, because even if you go to a Christian school, people still forget his Word and live in the flesh.

One day a friend of mine took me for a ride on his motorcycle. It was my first time on this monster bike. The thing weighs 600 pounds. I couldn't even hold it up if I had to. But he has been riding a long time—heck, he builds the things, he knows all about them, he's an expert in motorcycles—so I figured I'd be safe with him. As we were preparing for the ride, he gave me his pointers. Put on your helmet, hold on to me around the waist, and when we go into turns, lean into the turn. Okay, it all sounded fine. We started it up and took off. The road we were on was a windy one that wrapped around the mountains and hills of Oregon. When we got to the first big turn, the bike leaned over to the left. Instinctively, I started to lean the opposite way to keep the bike from falling over. I mean, we were practically tipped over. "Lean into it!" he shouted. I freaked and tried to lean in, but I just couldn't make myself do it. It seemed impossible. With everything in me I wanted to lean away from it to keep the bike from falling over, like I do when my car corners tightly. I wanted to distribute the weight so we wouldn't flip over.

My friend slowed down and pulled over to the shoulder. "You have to lean into the turn or I lose balance. You can't lean away from the turn. It's too dangerous." What he was saying made no sense to me, but it was true. If I did what I felt was right, we would crash. If I did what I was told to do, we would be fine. I would feel freaked, but I would be safe.

Following God's Word is kinda like that. It makes all the sense in the world till you have to actually do it when you're speeding down the highway at 55 miles per hour. Then it starts to seem dangerous. After all, if you love someone who hates you, they could really hurt you. In these trying times God's Word can seem preposterous. All he asks is, "Will you believe me even if the world says I'm lying to you, even if my commands seem dangerous?" And your only right response is, "Yes, I will." Any other answer would be outside of faith.

So what is his Word asking you to do right now? What does God require you to do in order to change this hungry planet? What will be your part in putting an end to meanness? If you want a world run by the precepts of Scripture, then *you are the one to help create it*. He has given you that desire so you will do something with it. Your faith isn't about what other girls are doing but about how you are responding to them. Will you falter in times of trouble and become like the Mean Girl, or will you rise above and believe God's Word no matter how preposterous it sounds?

> Your faith isn't about what other girls are doing but how you are responding to them.

I believe that your desire, just like mine, is to follow his teachings and to prove to yourself and to him that you trust him. And because of that, your life is going to change. Lucky for us, God never gives up on us. Even though we might have messed up in the past, he never throws his hands up in the air and walks away. He is ready to help us the moment we are ready to come back to him and trust him.

You might have been a Mean Girl in the past, or maybe just a girl who thought it was okay to get even. Either way, now is your chance to change. And when you've begun the change in yourself, then and only then can you begin to change the world around you. With these newfound truths and precepts, you have the ability, through the Holy Spirit, to change not just yourself but your entire school. One of my favorite quotes for reaching out to others is from the ancient book of Proverbs 24:11–12:

> Rescue those being led away to death; hold back those staggering toward slaughter. If you say, "But we knew nothing about this," does not he who weighs the heart perceive it? Does not he who guards your life know it? Will he not repay each person according to what he has done?

Now is your chance to rescue those who are staggering toward slaughter. If you don't do something to help the state of girls, do you expect God to look the other way? He has told you what he requires of you, and now you cannot say, "But we knew nothing about this." Until today you might not have known what was expected of you in relation to Mean Girls, but now you do, so now you are responsible for doing what you can to change your reactions to them and even to help change the reactions of others in your group and in your school. After all, if you don't do something, who will? You were made for a time such as this. You were made to rise above the others, and whatever the outcome, whatever the response, you can know that God is looking down at you and saying, "Well done, good and faithful servant." No matter what the outcome of our obedience on earth, we know that the outcome in heaven is blessings. God doesn't let your obedience go unrewarded.

I believe that today God is asking all of us to take back the feminine gender from the enemy. I believe he wants to start with this generation, to make you who you were intended to be: imitators of Christ, not the world. And I also believe that he has enlisted you as his soldier in this holy war. As a soldier you will need your orders and your weapons. In the rest of this book, you will find just what you need: explicit orders from the Commander as to how you are to operate on enemy territory, and the weapons you need to fight the battles that he will send you into. If you are ready, let's dive in.

The Battle Isn't against Flesh and Blood

Fight the Enemy, Not the Girl

I know you think your fight is against a girl. I know she's the one who is the thorn in your flesh right now, digging in and causing you all kinds of pain, but remember that things aren't always as they seem. And if you want a life filled with spiritual victories, then you've gotta learn one important thing: You aren't fighting the girl; you are fighting the enemy. Paul makes this totally clear in his letter to the Ephesians. Check this out.

> A final word: Be strong with the Lord's mighty power. Put on all of God's armor so that you will be able to stand firm against all strategies and tricks of the Devil. For we are not fighting against people made of flesh and blood, but against the evil rulers and authorities of the unseen world, against those mighty powers of darkness who rule this world, and against wicked spirits in the heavenly realms.
>
> Ephesians 6:10–12 NLT

See, you aren't fighting her, really. She's just the decoy, the thing that distracts you from the real issue. So take your eyes off of her, and let's get back to reality. It's like that movie *The Truman Show,* where Jim Carrey's character has no clue that he lives on a movie set and that everything he is doing is directed and planned by the show's producers and directors. It isn't till he steps outside the set that he can start to see the fakeness of all that he thought was reality. Take a look behind the scenes, just like Truman did, and see if you don't find out who's really pulling all the strings, writing all the lines, and making the mean actors play their parts. Don't hate the actors; hate the director who is directing them to be mean to you. For those of you who are having a blonde moment and have no idea who I am talking about, I mean Satan, the devil, the ruler of this earth. Check out 1 John 5:19 and 1 Peter 5:8–9. He's really the problem here—the director of evil.

Stand Firm

So if you aren't supposed to go after the actors, who do you go after and how do you do it? Well, first of all let's figure out our role in God's army. As I see it, we are never called to be on the offensive. We are only to defend. We defend our God, we defend the less fortunate, and we can defend ourselves against the attacks of the evil one, but never do we go in and pick a fight. It's called standing firm. You have three options in a fight: You can run away, you can go on the offensive and attack, or you can stand firm. Your call is to stand firm in who you are, what you believe, and Christ's commands to love your enemies. Remember that with him you are victorious. If you stand firm on a foundation that can't shake, then you don't have to run or attack, because you can simply stand. Jesus said, "By standing firm you will gain life" (Luke 21:19). And the apostle Paul tells us in 1 Corinthians 16:13, "Be on your guard; stand firm in the faith; be men of courage; be strong." In order to stand, you are called to be armored up and protected. That's why in Ephesians, Paul talks about us putting on the protective armor of God. We are called to suit up to protect our important parts—our minds, our hearts, and our feet. Check it out:

> Therefore put on the full armor of God, so that when the day of evil comes, you may be able to stand your ground, and after you have done everything, to stand. Stand firm then, with the belt of truth buckled around your waist, with the breastplate of righteousness in place, and with your feet fitted with the readiness that comes from the gospel of peace. In addition to all this, take up the shield of faith, with which you can extinguish all the flaming arrows of the evil one. Take the helmet of salvation and the sword of the Spirit, which is the word of God. And pray in the Spirit on all occasions with all kinds of prayers and requests.

With this in mind, be alert and always keep on praying for all the saints.

Ephesians 6:13–18

Your first step in fighting the real enemy is to suit up. Put on the right outfit to get ready for battle. You gotta have the right clothes on for the right occasion. I mean, you wouldn't go to school in your bathing suit or to the beach in your school clothes. And you don't go into battle without your spiritual armor. You can and should put it on every day. And I know you may have heard this a million times, but have you ever heard *how* to do it? It's not like you have a closet at home with all this stuff in it. So let's go over the list and how you put this stuff on. Every day you should ask God to dress you up in the following:

The helmet of salvation—The helmet protects your thoughts from the arrows the enemy will throw at you. Stuff like, You aren't good enough for God. He'll never forgive you for that. You have to work harder to make him love you. How do you even know he exists? Have you ever seen him? If you've ever had thoughts like these, then you need the helmet of salvation. It protects you by letting you know that you are saved, period, no matter what you do or how you do. No matter if you mess up or anything. You are saved, period. So with the helmet on, this tactic from the enemy is kaput.

The breastplate of righteousness—The breastplate was a defensive weapon that men wore in Bible times. Think of it like a metal corset. It protects your most important part, your heart. When the enemy starts to come at you with all kinds of lies about how bad you are, the breastplate stops that nonsense from getting into your heart. See, you *are* righteous just because he made you to be, not from anything you've done. God said there is no one righteous, not one, on their own (Romans 3:10). But you are righteous because *he* is righteous and *he* made you that way (see Romans 3:22). So Satan is lying when he tells you that you are no good. The breastplate of righteousness reminds you of that important fact.

The shield of faith—When a soldier went into battle, he always had a shield with him. That's the thing he held in his hand to deflect blows from spears, sword, and arrows. For believers our shield is our faith. It deflects all kinds of weapons from the enemy. Faith is what makes us win. It's what reminds us that we *do* win because Christ made it so (see 1 John 3:8, the second half of the verse). Without faith, don't dare go into battle, because you will certainly lose. Faith that God will protect you, that he works everything out for good, and that he is in control protects you from all kinds of stuff.

The belt of truth—The next little piece of apparel is your belt. It's essential. The belt of truth reminds you what's true, because the enemy's biggest weapon is the lie. He uses lies very masterfully to deceive you. He makes them look really close to the truth but just off enough to mess you up royally. If you have the belt of truth on, you will be able to distinguish the truth from a lie. And you won't fall for the lies of the enemy anymore (see 2 Corinthians 11:14 and John 8:44).

The sandals of the gospel of peace—The most important thing for us to know as believers is the gospel, the message of Jesus. Do you know the gospel? Can you tell someone the gospel on cue? It's crucial that you can. It's what saves you and everyone else on earth. Make sure that you know the gospel: the truth that there is no one righteous, not even one (Romans 3:10), and because of that a sacrifice had to be made for our sins. Christ was that sacrifice, once and for all. He died for our sins, even though he was sinless, so that we could have a right relationship with God. Without his death on the cross and resurrection, none of us would be saved. The old, some say overused verse John 3:16 is not just a cliché.

The sword of the Spirit—No warrior would be complete without his sword. This is used for hand-to-hand combat with the enemy. When they are in your face and you need to react to protect yourself, you pull out your sword. As a believer, your sword is God's Spirit, or his Word. You have to protect yourself with God's Word. The stuff he says in Scripture is so powerful that it can destroy the enemy. Don't just believe me; give it a try yourself. The next time you are thinking stupid or negative thoughts, pull out your favorite Scripture. Read it over and over again. Let the enemy know that he's a loser, you're the winner. Your team wins, and you are sure of it. The sword is a must if you want to fight the battle against the enemy.

Every morning before you leave the house, put on the right outfit. Make putting on your spiritual outfit more important than anything else you do. It doesn't take long. Just pray something like this:

Father, this morning I want to put on the armor of God. I want to put on the helmet of salvation so that I will remember that I am saved for good, and no one can take me away from you. It's permanent, this salvation thing. Thank you, Father. And I also want to put on the breastplate of righteousness. I know that I am righteous because you say I am. I am righteous because your Son died for me to make me righteous (Romans 4:22–25). I won't let the enemy lie to me about my sins or my faults, because it's none of his business. Next I want to put on the belt of truth around my waist. Your Word is true, and I know the truth will protect me. Today I will not tell myself lies or even let myself think about them. I'll only think what's true and excellent and good (Philippians 4:8).

Father, please put the sandals of the gospel of peace on my feet so that I will remember to tell those who don't know you the truth that Christ's death on a cross meant something. It meant that you loved each of us enough to give your Son for us. And because of that, nothing anyone says or does to me today will derail me. Thank you for the gift of the gospel.

The Gospel =

1. God loves you and has big plans for your life. (John 3:16; John 10:10)
2. Man is sinful, so man can't get close to God, who is all good. (Romans 3:23; Romans 6:23)
3. Jesus died and rose again so that we can get to God. He makes us righteous. He is the final sacrifice for each of us. (Romans 5:8; 1 Corinthians 15:3–6; John 14:6)
4. If you accept Christ as your sacrifice and make him Lord, then you can know God and live the big plans he has for you. (John 1:12; Ephesians 2:8–9; John 3:1–8)**

Father, I pick up the shield of faith and hold it with me no matter where I go today. My faith is secure. You are who you say you are, and no one can make me budge with the shield in my arms. Thank you for your protection for those who love you (1 Peter 1:5).

And last but not least, I'm picking up the sword of the Spirit to help me fight the enemy at every turn. The sword that you give me is your Word, the Bible. I will take it with me no matter where I go. I will learn verses that I know can fight the enemy, and if I can't remember them, I will write them down so I can take them wherever I go. Thanks for the protection and power of your words (Proverbs 7:2–3; Isaiah 54:17).

Thank you for the protection of your armor. Amen.

If you put on the armor of God every day, just like Paul teaches us in God's Word, then you will feel God's protection on you all day long. It's a good reminder of what is important too. If you can just remember the big stuff, like Jesus dying because of how much he loves you, then the other stuff gets kinda little in comparison. Don't let yourself ever forget the important truth of the gospel. It's your lifeline. It's your salvation. It's your only hope and all the hope in the world.

A Fight to the Finish

Check out how Eugene Peterson puts this section of Paul's letter to the Ephesians in *The Message:*

And that about wraps it up. God is strong, and he wants you strong. So take everything the Master has set out for you, well-made weapons of the best materials. And put them to use so you will be able to stand up to everything the Devil throws your way. This is no afternoon athletic contest that we'll walk away from and forget about in a couple of hours. This is for keeps, a life-or-death fight to the finish against the Devil and all his angels.

Be prepared. You're up against far more than you can handle on your own. Take all the help you can get, every weapon God has issued, so that when it's all over but the shouting you'll still be on your feet. Truth, righteousness, peace, faith, and salvation are more than words. Learn how to apply them. You'll need them throughout your life. God's Word is an indispensable weapon. In the same way, prayer is essential in this ongoing warfare. Pray hard and long. Pray for your brothers and sisters. Keep your eyes open. Keep each other's spirits up so that no one falls behind or drops out.

Ephesians 6:10–18 MESSAGE

Pray the Mean Out

You don't have the power to change people, but you do have the power to pray to the God who can. If you have allowed God to start cleaning you up to be holy in how you deal with Mean Girls yourself, then you can start to work toward cleaning up your school spiritually. A lot of what you've learned in this book will set you on the road to healing your school, but if you want to take it a step further, think about the fact that there is power in numbers. Jesus said,

> Again, I tell you that if two of you on earth agree about anything you ask for, it will be done for you by my Father in heaven.
>
> Matthew 18:19

Since Jesus said "anything," that must include the Mean Girls at your school. See if you can't find some other believers who want to honor God and start to pray the meanness out of your school. Get together once or twice a week before school or whatever works for you. Band together to lift your school up to God and watch what he does. You just need two or more willing to pray.

So what does prayer look like at your school? Let me first start by telling you what it doesn't look like:

1. No gossip—Prayer is not an opp to gossip. Don't use your prayer time to tell other girls the terrible things that are going on. Don't mention them. Your job isn't to spread more gossip; it's to stop it. So no talking about what bad things other girls are doing.

2. No cliques—If your prayer group becomes a clique, you are way off. No one should be excluded, or you'll be behaving just like the rest of those Mean Girls.

3. **Don't give up if you don't see a change—**
Remember, God's timing is flawless. He might not do things according to your demands, but it isn't your job to care about that. If you pray only because you demand results, your prayer will soon die because you won't be getting your way. Prayer is just as much about changing you and your spirit as it is about changing the object of prayer. So go to God in faith and rest in the fact that whatever the outcome, all is well. "Your will be done on earth as it is in heaven" (Matthew 6:10).

Now that we've gone through the don't-do list, let's think about some ways that you can use prayer to improve the female community around you:

1. **Pray Scripture—**The Bible is full of truth, and that truth spoken out loud is extremely powerful. Use God's Word to tell him what you want for your Mean Girl. Pray for your school, your home, your work, or wherever you deal with meanness. You'll find tons of Scriptures throughout this book and at the end, so check them out and find some of your own.

2. **Memory verse—**Take it a step further and decide on a memory verse or two that each of you will learn and carry with you. Put it on your notebooks and lockers. Memorize it and live it. (Check out the book of Proverbs 7:3.)

3. **Get your faith in action—**James tells us that faith without works is dead (James 2:17). So make it a part of your ritual to put into practice the things you pray for. As James Allen said, "Not what he wishes and prays for does a man get, but what he justly earns. His wishes and prayers are only gratified and answered when they harmonize with his thoughts and actions." Figure out ways to put verses into action. Here are some to get you started.

a. *Verse:* "Do not conform any longer to the pattern of this world, but be transformed by the renewing of your mind. Then you will be able to test and approve what God's will is—his good, pleasing and perfect will" (Romans 12:2). *Action:* Change the way you think. Renew your mind to think like God and help the rest of your group to do the same. Risk caring for others. If a Mean Girl is attacking another girl, come to her aid. Be there for her. Take her away from the attack or say something nice about her.

b. *Verse:* "If you confess with your mouth, 'Jesus is Lord,' and believe in your heart that God raised him from the dead, you will be saved" (Romans 10:9). *Action:* Tell girls about the amazing life and death of your Savior. Love them enough to want to save them from the gates of hell.

c. *Verse:* "For God did not give us a spirit of timidity, but a spirit of power, of love and of self-discipline" (2 Timothy 1:7). *Action:* Dare to make friends with the odd girl out, the one no one quite gets or even wants to be around. Become her friend.

d. *Verse:* "A generous man will himself be blessed, for he shares his food with the poor" (Proverbs 22:9). *Action:* Change your focus from worrying about gossip and mean to serving God. Volunteer in your community or, if you have extra cash, talk to a teacher about giving money anonymously to students who need it.

e. *Verse:* "A cheerful heart is good medicine, but a crushed spirit dries up the bones" (Proverbs 17:22). *Action:* Be happy. A smile can be a great gift to give someone, especially if they are dealing with Mean Girls. Some people might go a whole week without seeing anyone smile at them. Believe God's Word and give from it generously.

4. **Bible study**—Go through a *Mean Girls* Bible study with your friends, mom, sister, or whoever. Start to spread the news to this hungry planet about a life lived for God and free of mean. See www.meangirls.net for more info.

5. **The G.G.U. Contract**—Gather a group of girls to sign the Girl Grown Up Contract at the end of this book, and then hold each other accountable to your promise.

Leave No Mean Girl Behind (For Advanced Readers Only)

Here is the challenge and battle cry for those of you who feel you have this down: Leave no Mean Girl behind! Let's rescue them one by one. Let's refuse to fan the flame of their anger but instead let's nurture the love of their hearts. This might be the hardest thing you've ever done, but the rewards can be amazing.

Earlier in this book I asked you to imagine a world where girls didn't fight each other and where they weren't consumed with getting even or making life miserable for girls who have more than them. It seems like a pipe dream, I know, but I believe that if every girl reading this book could infect 2 other girls with this message and those 2 could infect 2 more and so on and so on, we could significantly change a generation of females.

This is something that has yet to be done. Right now, girls are mean in every generation. But I believe this is something the Holy Spirit wants from us, especially as the family of believers. All of his words point to this. Imagine if your sisterhood of believers were all G.G.U.'s and we didn't have a Mean Girl among us. Think how that would look to the outside world. Girls would really want to know more about this Christ who makes girls happy. So your challenge, should you choose to accept it, is to infect at least 2 other girls with this message and encourage them to do the same.

Log on to www.meangirls.net to find more girls who are taking the Mean Girl challenge. Compare notes. Start a revolution. Help make your generation the first generation of girls who aren't Mean Girls.

Ammo
for the
Battle

The Girl Grown Up Contract for the G.G.U.

The list in the chapter *The Girl Grown Up* (page 134) told you what a G.G.U. is. If you agree with that list and want to start today to live it, then here's the next step: the Girl Grown Up Contract. This is a contract between you and God to be signed in the presence of other sisters in Christ. Agree to hold each other accountable to it. Use the verses that go with it as a memory verse list to keep you on track. You can cut this contract out and keep it or hang it somewhere you'll see it to help you remember your commitment. And you can go to www.meangirls.net for a downloadable contract if you need copies for all your G.G. friends. Are you ready to be mean-free forever?

Begin with this prayer of commitment:

Father God, I am so much like Paul, who said, "I decide one way, but then I act another, doing things I absolutely despise. So if I can't be trusted to figure out what is best for myself and then do it, it becomes obvious that God's command is necessary" (Romans 7:15–16, *The Message* paraphrase). I don't like this side of me, but I know it exists, so I say thank you for Jesus and his death on the cross. I am not worthy, but I accept your free gift of salvation. I'm tired of using all my energy to say no to sin, so I will concentrate on saying yes to you and allow you to say no to sin for me. Father, I want to find out what pleases you and do it. In this book I have read about many things that you want us to do, and now I am ready to do them. So today I commit to this list. Help me keep my commitment. Thank you that you always do help me in my weakness. Amen.

My Girl Grown Up Contract

I, _____, enter into this contract on this day of ____
_____, 200_, for the purpose of glorifying God with my heart, mind, and actions. To this end I commit to take the following steps to make my little chunk of this planet a better place for all girls.

By signing this contract, I agree to the following conditions:

1. **I will love others more than myself.** "Jesus replied, 'You must love the Lord your God with all your heart, all your soul, and all your mind.' This is the first and greatest commandment. A second is equally important: 'Love your neighbor as yourself'" (Matthew 22:37–39 NLT).

2. **I will not gossip.** "Don't pass on malicious gossip" (Exodus 23:1 MESSAGE).

3. **I won't seek revenge.** "Do not take revenge, my friends, but leave room for God's wrath, for it is written: 'It is mine to avenge; I will repay,' says the Lord" (Romans 12:19).

4. **I will be gentle of spirit, not religious and legalistic.** "[Your beauty] should be . . . the unfading beauty of a gentle and quiet spirit, which is of great worth in God's sight" (1 Peter 3:4).

5. **I will laugh at myself.** "Obviously, I'm not trying to be a people pleaser! No, I am trying to please God. If I were still trying to please people, I would not be Christ's servant" (Galatians 1:10 NLT).

6. **I will care for others.** "Love never gives up. Love cares more for others than for self" (1 Corinthians 13:4 MESSAGE).

7. **I will hold other G.G.U.'s accountable.** "Share each other's troubles and problems, and in this way obey the law of Christ" (Galatians 6:2 NLT).

8. **I will forgive.** "If you forgive those who sin against you, your heavenly Father will forgive you" (Matthew 6:14 NLT).

9. **I will be happy when other girls win.** Love "doesn't revel when others grovel, takes pleasure in the flowering of truth, puts up with anything, trusts God always, always looks for the best, never looks back, but keeps going to the end" (1 Corinthians 13:6–7 MESSAGE).

10. **I will do all I can to leave others feeling good about themselves.** "Watch the way you talk. Let nothing foul or dirty come out of your mouth. Say only what helps, each word a gift" (Ephesians 4:29 MESSAGE).

_____
(your name)

The Sword of the Spirit—Using God's Word to Fight the Mean

If you don't want to become a Mean Girl by fighting back, these verses will be your guide. Don't let yourself get dragged into her vicious cycle of mean. It's not who you are, and it's not who you were made to be. Honor God and honor yourself by following his Word even in times of testing. Fight off the urge to fight back.

Anger

A fool gives full vent to his anger, but a wise man keeps himself under control.

Proverbs 29:11 NIV

A man's wisdom gives him patience; it is to his glory to overlook an offense.

Proverbs 19:11 NIV

Cliques

Playing favorites is always a bad thing; you can do great harm in seemingly harmless ways.

Proverbs 28:21 MESSAGE

Clothes

What matters is not your outer appearance—the styling of your hair, the jewelry you wear, the cut of your clothes—but your inner disposition. Cultivate inner beauty, the gentle, gracious kind that God delights in. The holy women of old were beautiful before God that way, and were good, loyal wives to their husbands. Sarah, for instance, taking care of Abraham, would address him as "my dear husband." You'll be true daughters of Sarah if you do the same, unanxious and unintimidated.

1 Peter 3:3–6 MESSAGE

Complaining/Criticizing

Friends, don't complain about each other. A far greater complaint could be lodged against you, you know. The Judge is standing just around the corner.

James 5:9 MESSAGE

You, therefore, have no excuse, you who pass judgment on someone else, for at whatever point you judge the other, you are condemning yourself, because you who pass judgment do the same things.

Romans 2:1 NIV

You didn't think, did you, that just by pointing your finger at others you would distract God from seeing all your misdoings and from coming down on you hard?

Romans 2:3 MESSAGE

Confess

If we confess our sins, he is faithful and just and will forgive us our sins and purify us from all unrighteousness.

1 John 1:9 NIV

He who covers his transgressions will not prosper, but whoever confesses and forsakes his sins will obtain mercy.

Proverbs 28:13 AMP

Cussing

But you know better now, so make sure it's all gone for good: bad temper, irritability, meanness, profanity, dirty talk. Don't lie to one another. You're done with that old life. It's like a filthy set of ill-fitting clothes you've stripped off and put in the fire. Now you're dressed in a new wardrobe. Every item of your new way of life is custom-made by the Creator, with his label on it. All the old fashions are now obsolete.

Colossians 3:8–10 MESSAGE

Fear

And God, in his mighty power, will protect you until you receive this salvation, because you are trusting him. It will be revealed on the last day for all to see.

1 Peter 1:5 NLT

"Though the mountains be shaken and the hills be removed, yet my unfailing love for you will not be shaken nor my covenant of peace be removed," says the LORD, who has compassion on you.

Isaiah 54:10 NIV

The LORD Almighty is the one you are to regard as holy, he is the one you are to fear, he is the one you are to dread.

Isaiah 8:13 NIV

Fighting

It is to a man's honor to avoid strife, but every fool is quick to quarrel.

Proverbs 20:3 NIV

The acts of the sinful nature are obvious: sexual immorality, impurity and debauchery; idolatry and witchcraft; hatred, discord, jealousy, fits of rage, selfish ambition, dissensions, factions and envy; drunkenness, orgies, and the like. I warn you, as I did before, that those who live like this will not inherit the kingdom of God. But the fruit of the Spirit is love, joy, peace, patience, kindness, goodness, faithfulness, gentleness and self-control. Against such things there is no law.

Galatians 5:19–23 NIV

If you are offering your gift at the altar and there remember that your brother has something against you, leave your gift there in front of the altar. First go and be reconciled to your brother; then come and offer your gift. Settle matters quickly with your adversary who is taking you to court.

Matthew 5:23–25 NIV

Forgiveness

Don't be in a hurry to go to court. You might go down before your neighbors in shameful defeat. So discuss the matter with them privately. Don't tell anyone else.

Proverbs 25:8–9 NLT

Friends

Disregarding another person's faults preserves love; telling about them separates close friends.

Proverbs 17:9 NLT

A friend loves at all times, and a brother is born for adversity.

Proverbs 17:17 NIV

Wounds from a friend can be trusted, but an enemy multiplies kisses.

Proverbs 27:6 NIV

Geeks

He who oppresses the poor shows contempt for their Maker, but whoever is kind to the needy honors God.

Proverbs 14:31 NIV

Gossips, Backstabbers, and Other Blabbermouths

So get rid of all malicious behavior and deceit. Don't just pretend to be good! Be done with hypocrisy and jealousy and backstabbing.

1 Peter 2:1 NLT

If you are insulted because of the name of Christ, you are blessed, for the Spirit of glory and of God rests on you. If you suffer, it should not be as a murderer or thief or any other kind of criminal, or even as a meddler. However, if you suffer as a Christian, do not be ashamed, but praise God that you bear that name. For it is time for judgment to begin with the family of God; and if it begins with us, what will the outcome be for those who do not obey the gospel of God?

1 Peter 4:14–17 NIV

A gossip betrays a confidence; so avoid a man who talks too much.

Proverbs 20:19 NIV

Please be quiet! That's the smartest thing you could do.

Job 13:5 NLT

Do not spread false reports. Do not help a wicked man by being a malicious witness.

Exodus 23:1 NIV

Humility

For by the grace given me I say to every one of you: Do not think of yourself more highly than you ought, but rather think of yourself with sober judgment, in accordance with the measure of faith God has given you.

Romans 12:3 NIV

A man's pride brings him low, but a man of lowly spirit gains honor.

Proverbs 29:23 NIV

Do not make friends with a hot-tempered man, do not associate with one easily angered.

Proverbs 22:24 NIV

Lying

Do not testify against your neighbor without cause, or use your lips to deceive.

Proverbs 24:28 NIV

Whoever of you loves life and desires to see many good days, keep your tongue from evil and your lips from speaking lies. Turn from evil and do good; seek peace and pursue it. The eyes of the LORD are on the righteous and his ears are attentive to their cry; the face of the LORD is against those who do evil, to cut off the memory of them from the earth.

Psalm 34:12–16 NIV

Telling lies about others is as harmful as hitting them with an ax, wounding them with a sword, or shooting them with a sharp arrow.

Proverbs 25:18 NLT

Mean Girls

Therefore, rid yourselves of all malice and all deceit, hypocrisy, envy, and slander of every kind.

1 Peter 2:1 NIV

Summing up: Be agreeable, be sympathetic, be loving, be compassionate, be humble. That goes for all of you, no exceptions. No retaliation. No sharp-tongued sarcasm. Instead, bless—that's your job, to bless. You'll be a blessing and also get a blessing.

1 Peter 3:8–9 MESSAGE

This suffering is all part of what God has called you to. Christ, who suffered for you, is your example. Follow in his steps. He never sinned, and he never deceived anyone. He did not retaliate when he was insulted. When he suffered, he did not threaten to get even. He left his case in the hands of God, who always judges fairly.

1 Peter 2:21–23 NLT

Let us not become weary in doing good, for at the proper time we will reap a harvest if we do not give up. Therefore, as we have opportunity, let us do good to all people, especially to those who belong to the family of believers.

Galatians 6:9–10 NIV

But now I am writing you that you must not associate with anyone who calls himself a brother but is sexually immoral or greedy, an idolater or a slanderer, a drunkard or a swindler. With such a man do not even eat.

1 Corinthians 5:11 NIV

Offended

We should please others. If we do what helps them, we will build them up in the Lord. For even Christ didn't please himself. As the Scriptures say, "Those who insult you are also insulting me."

Romans 15:2–3 NLT

Bless those who persecute you; bless and do not curse.

Romans 12:14 NASB

Revenge

Don't hit back; discover beauty in everyone. If you've got it in you, get along with everybody. Don't insist on getting even; that's not for you to do. "I'll do the judging," says God. "I'll take care of it."

Romans 12:17–19 MESSAGE

Do not make evil plans to harm each other.

Zechariah 7:10 NLT

Finally, all of you should be of one mind, full of sympathy toward each other, loving one another with tender hearts and humble minds. Don't repay evil for evil. Don't retaliate when people say unkind things about you. Instead, pay them back with a blessing. That is what God wants you to do, and he will bless you for it.

1 Peter 3:8–9 NLT

I will take vengeance; I will repay those who deserve it. In due time their feet will slip. Their day of disaster will arrive, and their destiny will overtake them.

Deuteronomy 32:35 NLT

Self-Control

A person without self-control is as defenseless as a city with broken-down walls.

Proverbs 25:28 NLT

It is better to be patient than powerful; it is better to have self-control than to conquer a city.

Proverbs 16:32 NLT

Spiritual Warfare

We use God's mighty weapons, not mere worldly weapons, to knock down the Devil's strongholds. With these weapons we break down every proud argument that keeps people from knowing God. With these weapons we conquer their rebellious ideas, and we teach them to obey Christ. And we will punish those who remained disobedient after the rest of you became loyal and obedient.

2 Corinthians 10:4–6 NLT

For we are not fighting against people made of flesh and blood, but against the evil rulers and authorities of the unseen world, against those mighty powers of darkness who rule this world, and against wicked spirits in the heavenly realms.

Ephesians 6:12 NLT

But in that coming day, no weapon turned against you will succeed. And everyone who tells lies in court will be brought to justice. These benefits are enjoyed by the servants of the LORD; their vindication will come from me. I, the LORD, have spoken!

Isaiah 54:17 NLT

Suffering

Endure suffering along with me, as a good soldier of Christ Jesus. And as Christ's soldier, do not let yourself become tied up in the affairs of this life, for then you cannot satisfy the one who has enlisted you in his army. Follow the Lord's rules for doing his work, just as an athlete either follows the rules or is disqualified and wins no prize. Hardworking farmers are the first to enjoy the fruit of their labor.

2 Timothy 2:3–6 NLT

Of course, you get no credit for being patient if you are beaten for doing wrong. But if you suffer for doing right and are patient beneath the blows, God is pleased with you.

1 Peter 2:20 NLT

The truth is, a kernel of wheat must be planted in the soil. Unless it dies it will be alone—a single seed. But its death will produce many new kernels—a plentiful harvest of new lives.

John 12:24 NLT

Yet what we suffer now is nothing compared to the glory he will give us later.

Romans 8:18 NLT

Thoughts

Above all else, guard your heart, for it affects everything you do.

Proverbs 4:23 NLT

Worry weighs a person down; an encouraging word cheers a person up.

Proverbs 12:25 NLT

And now, dear brothers and sisters, let me say one more thing as I close this letter. Fix your thoughts on what is true and honorable and right. Think about things that are pure and lovely and admirable. Think about things that are excellent and worthy of praise.

Philippians 4:8 NLT

Worry

Give all your worries and cares to God, for he cares about what happens to you.

1 Peter 5:7 NLT

But make up your mind not to worry beforehand how you will defend yourselves. For I will give you words and wisdom that none of your adversaries will be able to resist or contradict.

Luke 21:14–15 NIV

Ignoring what they said, Jesus told the synagogue ruler, "Don't be afraid; just believe."

Mark 5:36 NIV

Rejoice in the Lord always. I will say it again: Rejoice! Let your gentleness be evident to all. The Lord is near. Do not be anxious about anything, but in everything, by prayer and petition, with thanksgiving, present your requests to God.

Philippians 4:4–6 NIV

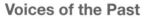

Voices of the Past

You can find holy thoughts in places other than the Bible. Many godly men and women have done and said amazing things over the centuries. Check out these thoughts that will help you fight the urge to fight back.

Let a man cease from his harsh thoughts, and all the world will soften towards him.

James Allen

I do not like to think of you as needing to have "things" pleasant around you when you have God within you. Surely He is enough to content any soul. If He is not enough here, how will it be in the future life when we have only Him Himself?

Hannah Whitall Smith

By your mind's confession, you condemn yourself.

Tertullian

If we think of dishonorable things we are evil.

Athanasius

The antithesis of giving thanks is grumbling. The grumblers live in state of self-induced stress.

Brennan Manning

Speak only when it would be sinful to be silent.

Sulpitius Severus

All sin is committed by our desire for good life and our fear of pain. But the things we do for a good life are lies that make us even more miserable than ever before.

Augustine

The Lord doesn't allow unthankful people to have peace.

Athanasius

If any outburst of anger takes place, the Holy Spirit seeks to depart because He does not have a pure place. For the Lord dwells in patience, but the devil in anger.

Hermas

Whatever man feels deeply or images clearly, is impressed upon the subconscious mind, and carried out in minutest detail.

Florence Scovel Shinn

To live continually in thoughts of cynicism, suspicion, and envy, is to be confined in a self-made prison.

James Allen

When anyone provokes you, remember that it is your own opinion about him that provokes you. Try not to be tossed around by appearances.

Epectitus

Nothing touches our lives but it is God Himself speaking. Do we discern His hand or only mere occurrence? Get into the habit of saying, "Speak, Lord," and life will become a romance. Every time circumstances press, say, "Speak, Lord"; make time to listen. Chastening is more than a means of discipline, it is meant to get me to the place of saying, "Speak, Lord."

Oswald Chambers

Obstinacy and self-will will always stab Jesus Christ. It may hurt no one else, but it wounds His Spirit. Whenever we are obstinate and self-willed and set upon our own ambitions, we are hurting Jesus. Every time we stand on our rights and insist that this is what we intend to do, we are persecuting Jesus.

Oswald Chambers

Never shall you come into such a position that Christ cannot aid you. No pinch shall ever arrive in your spiritual affairs in which Jesus Christ shall not be equal to the emergency, for your history has all been foreknown and provided for in Jesus.

Charles Spurgeon, *Morning and Evening*

Choosing Christ

As you should have figured out by now, none of what we've talked about in this book is possible without God. But there is a bonus: His love for you is about more than just saving you from the Mean Girl; it's about saving you too. If you want hope, purpose, and reason in your life, you will find it all when you get to know God. And if you don't know him right now, here is your chance. If you are tired of living life on your own power without all of these assurances that you've read about, then pray this simple prayer right now, and God will give you this life-changing power absolutely free.

> If you confess with your mouth that Jesus is Lord and believe in your heart that God raised him from the dead, you will be saved. For with the heart one believes and is justified, and with the mouth one confesses and is saved.
>
> Romans 10:9–10 ESV

Dear God, I thought I knew who you were, but I don't think I ever did. I've been living my life the way I wanted, and I'm not doing such a good job. I know that I can't do it myself anymore. I need you. I want you. I confess that I've done most of it all wrong, and now I want to do it right. I trust what the Bible says about you, and I want to be obedient to it. I trust you to save me and to give me eternal life. I believe that Jesus Christ died for me on the cross so that my sins can be forgiven if I just believe. So today, God, I tell you that I accept Christ as my Savior and want to make him Lord of my life. Thank you for loving me. I love you, Lord. Amen.

Hayley DiMarco has written books including *Dateable, The Dateable Rules,* and *The Dirt on Breaking Up.* Her authority for answers to life's most pressing questions comes from the Word of God. Her goal is to give practical answers for life's problems from God's Word and disciple girls and women into a stronger life of faith. From working for a little shoe company called Nike to traveling the world with a French theater troupe, Hayley has seen a lot of life and decided that God's way is the only way that makes sense. Hayley is the president of Hungry Planet, a group that feeds the world's appetite for truth through authors and speakers taking on biblical issues with a distinctly modern voice.

This year her *Dateable* expertise (and of course prayers!) paid off, and she found the man of her dreams. Hayley Morgan became Hayley DiMarco on January 1. Yee ha! Both Hayley and her husband, Michael, now travel this hungry planet, speaking on issues of faith in life.

www.meangirls.net

Thanks to Michael for his faith and perseverance at keeping me on focus and to Wendy for being my favorite editor on the planet. Thanks to Jen for believing in my dream. Thanks to Katie for being so quick to help out and to Mom for giving me the confidence to follow my dreams. And finally, thanks to my Father for teaching me how to love Mean Girls.

Dateable fever is sweeping the nation!

Dateable:
are you?
are they?

Justin Lookadoo and Hayley

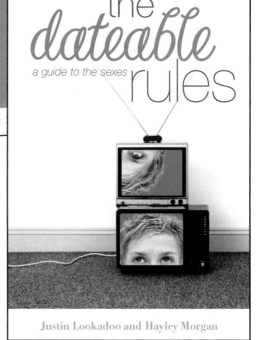

the
dateable
a guide to the sexes rules

Justin Lookadoo and Hayley Morgan

Are you missing out?

Nitty-gritty, tell-all honesty ...
you will love it!

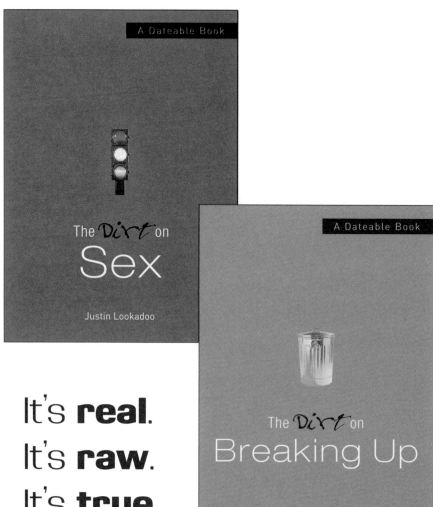

A Dateable Book

The *Dirt* on
Sex

Justin Lookadoo

A Dateable Book

The *Dirt* on
Breaking Up

Hayley DiMarco & Justin Lookadoo

It's **real**.
It's **raw**.
It's **true**.

It's the Dirt.

www.meangirls.net